North Carolina Auto Accident & Insurance Law

CARL NAGLE

Lulu Publishing Services rev. date: 08/29/2016

After working for years in the insurance industry, I felt a calling to educate and assist accident victims. Through this book, I offer my guidance and experience to victims of vehicle collisions. This work is dedicated to the wonderful clients who have allowed me to assist them through their medical recovery, and to help them resolve all financial and legal problems arising from motor vehicle accidents. Thank you dear clients for giving me the opportunity to serve you.

CONTENTS

FOREWORD

I dislike insurance companies. Through their advertising, they encourage us to trust them after an accident occurs. However, they remain detached and uncaring, and they only look to maximize profits for their executives and shareholders.

Before law school, I worked for several years as a claims adjuster for a large, national auto insurance company. I was trained to avoid payment of valid claims. Insurance adjusters are cost-control experts who will offer words of kindness and then pay you as little as you let them. Frankly, nice guys finish last when dealing with insurance adjusters after an accident.

I also worked as an insurance company lawyer defending at-fault drivers who faced valid lawsuits filed by accident victims. With my past experience, I can confirm that insurance companies always seek to minimize payment to innocent victims.

This book is offered to help level the playing field. Whether you hire an attorney or handle your case alone, you need to know the rules of the game before you can assess payment offers on all accident claims. Insurance companies hold on to *your* money by leveraging superior knowledge, by questioning valid claims, and by putting you in the uncomfortable position of defending your credibility. If you know your rights, you can meet the insurance adjusters on even ground. If you understand what you are entitled to and how to access multiple insurance policies to collect the *full* value of all allowable accident claims, you will not leave your money in the insurance company's bank account when your claim file is closed.

North Carolina collision law is quite complex. As a practicing attorney who only handles auto accident cases, I must caution you that no single book can provide complete legal advice to every accident victim. This book, however, will help you to prepare for your discussions with insurance adjusters. If you choose to hire an attorney, this work will help you understand all of the steps your attorney should take to earn his or her fee, to increase your settlement, or to collect full case value through a jury trial. If you handle your case without an attorney, this book will help you to confront most of the pitfalls and payment-avoidance techniques that adjusters use in every injury case.

Money is far less important than health, safety, and quality of life. However, money is the only focus for insurance companies and the adjusters who represent them. Insurance companies know that accident victims have legal rights and that the law allows the victim to collect money for various expenses and losses. While you seek to focus on recovering your health, the insurance adjusters are solely concerned with minimizing their financial obligations. From the first report of a covered accident, they begin collecting evidence that allows them either to deny your claims or to reduce what they owe. They will not openly explain what you can collect, and indeed, they will keep your money if you do not know what to ask for.

I truly hope this work helps you to understand your legal rights, your legal options, and your best plan of response following a motor vehicle accident. If you have questions about your rights or options or if you need help applying this text to your unique circumstances, I can be reached by telephone at (800) 411-1583 or online through www.naglefirm.com. No accident victim should feel alone when responding to a collision. This book provides immediate guidance, and I hope that you gain every advantage as you seek to protect your family's health, credit, and financial interests.

Carl Nagle

CHAPTER 1

❖

MONEY SOURCES FOR ACCIDENT VICTIMS

After an accident, one of the first questions you face is who will pay for your expenses and losses. A discussion of the sources of payment involves analysis of the various types of insurance policies that fund auto accident claims. While car insurance policies fund most claims, there are additional outside sources that must be considered in cases involving serious injuries and higher damages.

We will explore all of the sources that might provide payment to your family following an auto accident. We begin with a general discussion of the types of coverage provided through auto insurance policies: liability insurance, uninsured motorist coverage, underinsured motorist coverage, collision coverage, medical payments coverage, and personal injury protection. We will then look at non-auto-based insurance and other outside payment sources that provide essential additional payments to victims who suffer more serious injuries. Because duplicate payments are often allowed, victims should look at every money source as they seek full and fair payment for expenses and losses arising from a motor vehicle accident.

Auto-Insurance-Based Payment Sources and Coverage Types

In chapter 2, we look at the North Carolina standard form auto policy and discuss the basic legal principles of insurance. In this chapter our focus is on how each of the coverage types is triggered, and what the insurance companies owe under each section of the insurance policy. Since multiple coverages can often be accessed, each money source should be considered to determine whether duplicate coverage and duplicate payment of covered losses might be available.

Liability Insurance Coverage

Liability coverage protects other drivers and individuals if you cause an accident. This is mandatory coverage and will be part of every auto insurance policy issued in North Carolina.

Liability means "legally responsible." To collect from another driver's liability insurance, you must prove that the other driver was careless or negligent. You must also show that you did not contribute to causing the accident. Beware in North Carolina because our pure contributory negligence law is the most difficult negligence law in the country. If you are *slightly* at fault for the accident (even just 1 percent to blame), you have no claims or right of payment. Never admit blame or responsibility in discussions with insurance adjusters and other drivers.

Liability insurance follows the vehicle in North Carolina. If you are driving your own car, your personal auto policy will provide liability coverage if you cause an accident. If you are driving a borrowed car, the car owner's liability policy is first in line to pay for the damages caused to other parties. All victims will present their claims under the policy covering the at-fault vehicle. If multiple drivers and vehicles are responsible for causing the accident, claims can be presented against multiple policies. This allows you to add all available liability coverage together and increase the insurance money available to pay your claims.

> ### *Example*
>
> John and Andy are both driving separate vehicles and both enter the same intersection under a red light. Alice enters the intersection under a green light and is struck by John and Andy. Alice's injuries and losses are caused by the combined negligence of two drivers. Therefore, she can collect from John's liability policy *and* Andy's liability policy.

The two types of liability coverage found on every policy are property damage liability and bodily injury liability. Property damage coverage pays for all vehicle damage and other personal property loss. Bodily injury liability is separate coverage for physical injuries caused in the accident. Only innocent victims can collect, including other drivers and all innocent guest passengers. The coverage for bodily injury is typically split-limits, with a single per-person limit and a per-accident limit on the same policy. The per-person limit is the most any single victim can collect from that policy, regardless of the extent of medical care costs or the severity of injury. The per-accident limit is the most any group of victims will receive for all injury claims arising from a single accident or occurrence.

Liability coverage on auto policies is typically issued in the following amounts:

- property damage—$25,000.00
  bodily injury per victim / per occurrence—$30,000.00/$60,000.00
- property damage—$50,000.00
  bodily injury per victim / per occurrence—$50,000.00/$100,000.00
- property damage—$100,000.00
  bodily injury per victim / per occurrence—$100,000.00/$300,000.00
- property damage—$100,000.00
  bodily injury—$300,000.00 combined single limit
- property damage—$100,000.00
  bodily injury—per victim / per occurrence $250,000.00/$500,000.00
- property damage—$250,000.00
  bodily injury—per victim / per occurrence $500,000.00/$1,000,000.00

Advice on Buying Liability Insurance

If you cause an accident, you are personally responsible to pay for all vehicle damage, personal property damage, victim medical care costs, victim wage loss, and for all victims' pain and suffering. Car accidents cause serious injuries, and the victims' claims can easily exceed $100,000.00. If you do not purchase enough coverage, a victim can sue you and secure a verdict for the full value of all losses. If your insurance is not sufficient to pay the verdict in full, they can levy and take your bank accounts and personal property, place a judgment lien on your home, and collect the uninsured portion of their verdict from your personal wealth.

Always carry enough insurance. This determination depends in part on the personal wealth and assets you have to protect. We recommend that any driver carry *at least* $100,000.00 per person / $300,000.00 per occurrence in bodily injury liability coverage.

The cost of a single emergency room visit following a serious accident can approach the state's required minimum liability coverage limit. Thus, even if you have little wealth to protect, it costs very little to increase your coverage limits above the state minimums. If you carry sufficient coverage, you can trust that your insurance carrier will have sufficient resources to resolve almost any claim that follows a typical car accident.

Excess Liability Coverage—Accessing Multiple Auto Policies

Accident victims often fail to present their claims and collect under all available insurance policies! They leave their money in the insurance company's hands simply because they don't know where to look for additional coverage and benefits. If the insurance coverage on the vehicle is not sufficient to pay victim claims, it is essential to look carefully to identify hidden policies that will help to fund your claims.

Later in this chapter, we discuss excess liability coverage scenarios that do not involve auto insurance, including commercial/business liability insurance (which applies when an employee causes an accident during work hours) and homeowner's umbrella insurance. These nonauto sources are typically high-limits policies that provide a great deal of money to cover your losses and expenses. In serious and catastrophic injury cases, *always* look for these hidden policies, as they provide large money sources to cover your claims.

Example: Hidden Policy Pays $550,000.00!

We represented Carol F., who approached us following an accident. She and her husband had already secured a policy limits offer of $100,000.00. They simply wanted our advice to confirm that this was the only money available. After performing an asset search, we determined that the at-fault driver had very little wealth and no real estate to pursue. However, we looked closely at the collision facts and noticed that the at-fault driver was driving a late-model pickup truck at lunchtime near downtown Raleigh. On suspicion that he may have been employed, we compelled the liability insurer's legal representatives to secure a sworn affidavit from the at-fault driver disclosing the nature of his journey and his point of origin and destination, identifying his employer, and confirming whether he was within the scope of his employment when the crash occurred. After learning that he was employed, we were able to collect an additional $575,000.00 from the employer's commercial liability policy for Carol. Before they secured the advice of counsel, they were very close to signing a release limiting their payment to the initial/primary coverage. This release would have barred all additional claims. Thankfully, the hidden excess commercial policy paid over a half million dollars in additional benefits for Carol's family.

The most common excess liability scenario is the borrowed vehicle accident. Liability insurance follows the vehicle in North Carolina. If a driver borrows a nonowned vehicle and causes an accident, the first source for payment of victims' claims will be the vehicle owner's policy. If the owner's policy is insufficient to pay all losses, the driver's personal auto policy provides secondary or "excess" liability insurance. This coverage is called excess because it pays only after all coverage for the primary policy (the policy covering the at-fault vehicle) is paid out and exhausted.

Example

John borrows Andy's car to run errands. John causes an accident after he disregards a stop sign and collides with Alice. The primary policy covering Andy and Andy's car provides the state minimum mandatory liability coverage of $30,000.00 per person for bodily injury. John has his own car insurance with bodily injury liability coverage of $100,000.00 per person. The total liability insurance available to pay Alice's injury claims is $130,000.00. If Alice's injury claims are valued at $90,000.00, John's primary policy pays the first $30,000.00. Andy's personal auto policy provides excess liability coverage to pay the additional $60,000.00.

Another common excess liability scenario is the extra liability policy in the driver's household. The accident victim should request the policy information for every "family member" (person related by blood or marriage who resided with the at-fault driver on the accident date) whenever the value of the injury claim exceeds the coverage limit available on the policy that covers the at-fault vehicle. If the at-fault driver has his or her own policy, this coverage would be second in line behind the vehicle policy to pay victim losses. If these two policies are not sufficient to cover all injury claims, family members' auto liability policies will often provide additional, excess coverage to pay the victim's claims. Be sure to look for all coverage to ensure that your claims are paid in full.

Beware of any partial settlements in excess liability cases! If multiple liability policies protect the at-fault driver, you must settle your claim with one single settlement against all liability carriers. If you sign a release to collect under just the primary policy, this release waives and stops all claims against any available excess coverage. Whenever you are facing a policy limits settlement offer that does not fully pay your claims, take the time to scrutinize the collision facts, vehicle ownership facts, and the driver's employment and wealth before you accept the policy limits offer that leaves your losses only partially paid.

Uninsured Motorist Coverage

Uninsured motorist (UM) coverage pays the claims of all victims who are injured by a driver who failed to pay premiums and carry insurance and victims of hit-and-run drivers. Under the UM policy, you may claim payments for car and personal property damage under the uninsured motorist property damage (UMPD) coverage, and you can also collect for all injury claims under the uninsured motorist bodily injury (UMBI) coverage.

In hit-and-run cases, you cannot use the uninsured motorist coverage to pay for your property damage. This is unfortunate because the collision deductible is almost always higher than the standard $100.00 deductible that applies to UMPD claims. Also, in a hit-and-run accident, there must be a "hit," or some measure of contact with the at-fault vehicle. If there is no contact, these claims are called "phantom vehicle" cases. For example, if a driver crosses the center line and you leave the roadway to avoid the collision, and if you succeed in avoiding any impact and the other driver leaves the scene, you cannot use UM coverage to fund your accident claims. Essentially, you are left with no coverage for injury claims other than medical payments. This leaves the victim with no compensation for lost wages or for pain and suffering.

The more typical UM claim involves a driver who failed to make timely premium payments or failed to ever buy insurance and who later causes an accident. If you are injured by an uninsured driver, uninsured motorist coverage pays for your claims. Once the claim is closed, the insurance company that paid UM benefits can then sue the uninsured driver for reimbursement, and they can also suspend the uninsured driver's North Carolina driver's license.

UM coverage applies exactly the same way that liability coverage applies. You should not trust the UM adjusters to volunteer full and fair payment. Instead, you should expect them to oppose your claims. In fact, they will act just as though the uninsured driver was their insured/policyholder. They will question your claims and force you to provide recorded statements and medical history, and they will even hire a lawyer to defend the uninsured driver in court if a trial is necessary to secure fair payment for your injuries and losses.

If you present a claim for car replacement or repairs under your UM policy, the adjuster will pay fairly with little resistance. This is solely because our insurance regulations require fair payment on property damage claims. However, if you present an injury claim, you should be extremely careful in all discussions and dealings. The UM adjuster will always seek to minimize what they pay in every injury claim. Just remember that the UM adjuster represents the uninsured driver, *not* the victims or the policyholder who paid the premiums!

Don't Worry about Your Premiums

Many people resist using their own insurance when another driver causes their accident. However, if the other driver failed to carry liability insurance, UM coverage is the only way to collect for your injuries and losses. *Look out for liability defenses!* If you were slightly at fault for the accident, your UM adjuster owes nothing for your accident claims. Again, UM adjusters represent the uninsured driver, and they behave just as they would if you were presenting a claim under liability insurance. If you are slightly at fault, our harsh negligence laws disallow payment rights. Thus, expect the UM adjuster to place some blame with you if you were driving.

The good news is if you do receive payments through the UM policy, this confirms the insurer's determination that you did nothing wrong. Thus, if you collect under the UM policy, this will not cause any increase in your insurance premiums. Also, the insurance company will not drop your policy or discontinue future coverage.

Stacking Multiple UM Policies

If you are eligible for UM benefits, you can collect under multiple policies! North Carolina law allows interpolicy stacking of uninsured motorist (UM) and underinsured motorist (UIM) policies. Intrapolicy stacking, which refers to stacking coverage within the same policy, is not allowed. Thus, the focus in your search for coverage is whether there are different policies with different policy numbers that provide UM coverage in your case. Here are the types of policies that provide UM coverage to accident victims:

- UM policy for the vehicle you were riding in
- UM coverage on every car insurance policy that you own and which shows you as a "named insured" on the policy declarations
- UM policies for all "resident relatives"—here, you can collect under every policy in your household that insures any other driver who is related to you by blood or marriage.

You should search carefully for all applicable policies, and you can collect full benefits from each and every policy that applies.

Avoid Partial Settlements

If you have a large claim involving serious injury, never settle early and always make sure that every applicable UM policy is brought into the settlement discussions. Insurance adjusters want to settle your claims and close their file. They will not help you build your damages claim, find reasons why they should pay you more money, or help you to identify hidden coverage. Also, if you settle the UM claim with the obvious/ primary UM carrier, they will take a full release, which will block your right to collect additional UM payments from outside policies. Settle your claims only after you have looked at the complete medical picture, only after you have determined the likely verdict value of your injury case, and only after you have compelled all UM insurance carriers to apply all stackable policies to determine the total amount of coverage available in your case.

Example—UM Stacking

Alice is riding with her friend Sherry when an uninsured driver runs a red light and causes a serious collision. Sherry has UM coverage with bodily injury coverage limits of $30,000.00 per person. Alice lives in a separate residence and has her own car insurance policy with UMBI limits of $50,000.00 per person. Alice's husband owns a motorcycle and has his bike insurance under a separate policy with UMBI limits of $100,000.00 per person. Alice's mother-in-law, Mary, lives with them in the same residence, and Mary has her own auto insurance policy with UMBI limits of $50,000.00 per person. All of these policies can be accessed, and Alice therefore has a total of $230,000.00 to pay for her injury claims arising from her accident.

Advice on Buying Uninsured Motorist Coverage

Even though insurance is mandatory, many drivers fail to make their monthly payments and they lose their coverage. Unfortunately, accident victims often learn that the responsible driver did not carry insurance. This is why our legislature recently mandated uninsured motorist (UM) coverage on all auto policies.

UM coverage is very inexpensive! I recommend that you always carry at least $100,000.00 per person / $300,000.00 per occurrence for UM bodily injury. It costs very little to protect yourself and to ensure that there is sufficient money to pay your claims in full if you ever fall victim to an uninsured driver.

Underinsured Motorist Coverage

Underinsured motorists (UIM) coverage is very similar to uninsured motorist coverage. The only difference is it applies in cases where the at-fault vehicle *does* have liability insurance. UIM coverage is extra insurance available to pay your claims if the at-fault driver's liability insurance limits are lower than the UIM limits available under all policies. To determine if you can use the UIM coverage, you must look at all available liability policies and all available UIM policies. After adding together all per-person coverages for each type of policy, you compare the aggregate liability coverage limit to the aggregate UIM coverage limit. If the UIM limit is higher, you can collect additional benefits through the UIM policies. To determine the amount of UIM available, simply subtract the total available liability coverage from the total available UIM; the difference is the amount that the UIM coverage would pay above the liability policies.

Example: Calculating Available UIM Coverage

John enters an intersection under a red light and strikes Alice. John has liability coverage of $30,000.00 per person for bodily injury. Alice has a personal auto policy with UIM coverage limits of $100,000.00 per victim. Because John's coverage limits are *lower* than Alice's UIM limits, her UIM coverage is triggered. If her claims are worth $100,000.00, she collects the first $30,000.00 from John's liability policy and the remaining $70,000.00 from her policy.

Stacking UIM Policies

UIM coverage is stackable in North Carolina, and the coverage sources are identical to the coverage sources for UM shown above. If multiple policies are available for stacking, the liability limit is subtracted only once! To properly determine the amount of available coverage, you first identify all UIM policies available. After stacking all coverage and determining the total available UIM coverage amount, you then subtract the liability coverage amount from the total available limits.

Example: Using and Stacking UIM

John borrows Andy's car and causes an accident that injures Alice. Andy has a liability insurance policy with bodily injury coverage limits of $30,000.00 per person. John has his own car insurance with liability limits of $50,000.00 per person. Alice is driving her own car, and she has a UIM policy with a $50,000.00 per person limit. Alice's husband has a separate car insurance policy that also has UIM limits of $50,000.00 per person for bodily injury. Alice's daughter also resides with her, and she has another separate car insurance policy with UIM limits of $100,000.00 per person. Adding all liability limits together, we see there is a total of $80,000.00 in liability coverage to fund Alice's injury claims. The total of all available UIM policies that cover Alice would be $200,000.00. Therefore, Alice can collect up to $200,000.00 for all injury claims, with the first $80,000.00 paid through John's and Andy's liability coverage and the remaining $120,000.00 being paid through stackable UIM coverage.

Collision/Comprehensive Coverage

If another driver causes your accident, it is best to collect for car damage and personal property loss through their liability insurance policy. However, if you have collision coverage on your policy, you retain the option to have your vehicle repair or replacement cost paid through your own policy. While your payments would be reduced by the amount of your deductible, your insurance carrier will pursue reimbursement of their payout and your deductible once the collision claim is paid and closed. If the collision was partially your fault, collision coverage will be the only avenue of payment for vehicle damage.

Comprehensive coverage pays for vehicle damage caused by non-collision-based causes, such as storm damage, vandalism, and theft. In North Carolina, collision and comprehensive coverages are paired under the policy and carry the same deductible.

Medical Payments Coverage

Medical Payments (medpay) coverage is a portable health insurance policy that attaches to your auto insurance package. Medpay is purely optional coverage in North Carolina. It is very inexpensive, and I recommend that you always carry at least $5,000.00 in medpay coverage for all insured vehicles. The cost per vehicle for this coverage would only be approximately $8.00 per month. For that small premium, you have $5,000.00 in immediate coverage for all medical care arising from any car accident. This is a per-person limit and would apply for every passenger in your car. Further, medpay will pay your medical expenses even if you are riding with a friend in a car that is not insured on your policy, when struck by any vehicle while riding a bicycle, or when walking as a pedestrian and under multiple policies when medpay is available from several sources.

Don't Worry about Your Premiums

If you use medpay to collect for medical expenses arising from an accident that is not your fault, the medical payments claims will not impact your coverage or premiums. Thus, you will not face any additional costs or premium hikes if you collect the full amount of medpay available under your policy. If the accident was your fault, the accident (and not the medical payments claim filing) would result in an increase in premiums either way, but you would not face dropped coverage or any meaningful premium increase as a result of any medpay claim.

Medpay Coverage Allows Duplicate Payments

Medical payments coverage is not subject to rights of subrogation. This means that if you are able to collect your medical expenses through a liability claim against another driver who causes your accident, you do not have to reimburse your medpay carrier for their pay out. Thus, if you have $5,000.00 in medpay and they pay that total amount for your medical bills, you can collect again for the same medical expenses through your claims against the responsible driver's liability policy. You would not be required to reimburse your medpay carrier. Essentially, you are legally allowed to collect two times for your medical expenses in these cases. In fact, most health insurance coverage also overlaps with medical payments. If your health insurance is the type that does not have rights of subrogation and reimbursement, this would be a *third* source of payment and collection for medical expenses. Your attorneys will help you to apply overlapping coverages properly to ensure that you secure all insurance benefits available to you.

Available Medpay Coverage Options

Medpay coverage is typically sold in the following increments/amounts:

- $500.00 per person / per accident
- $1,000.00 per person / per accident
- $2,000.00 per person / per accident
- $5,000.00 per person / per accident
- $10,000.00 per person / per accident
- $25,000.00 per person / per accident
- $50,000.00 per person / per accident
- $100,000.00 per person / per accident

Because this coverage is very inexpensive and allows duplicate collection of medical-care costs for accident victims, we strongly recommend that you carry the highest medpay limit that you can afford.

Avoid Attorneys' Fees on Medpay

If you have medpay coverage and you undergo medical treatment for accident-related injuries, the insurance carrier is required to pay reasonable and necessary medical costs. The treatment must be medical in nature and indeed medically necessary. Also, the billed charges must be reasonable and customary for medical practitioners in the local medical community. Once these conditions are met, the medpay adjuster will pay medpay benefits to you or directly to your doctors.

While lawyers can charge a fee to present your medpay claims, I feel that the coverage is automatic and therefore my law firm files medpay claims for our clients free of charge. You should ask this of any attorney. If you must pay a fee, you may prefer to present your medpay claims alone and without counsel. In these cases, it is always best to use the medpay solely for unpaid medical expenses or as direct reimbursement to you for medical charges that you already paid. Proper use of medpay and careful priority of payment (e.g., pay EMS charges first, as they can garnish wages and impact personal credit faster than other medical bills) will allow you to maximize your net share of the personal injury settlement, protect your personal credit, and allow you access to more medical treatment options.

Stacking and Accessing Multiple Medical Payments Policies

If you have your own personal auto policy, your medpay coverage will always provide benefits unless you are driving a vehicle that you own or that is furnished for your regular use *and* that is not insured on the same policy that provides medpay coverage. Other than your own policy, you may also look to the following sources of medpay and collect from multiple policies to increase benefits available to pay accident-related medical costs:

- The auto policy for any non-owned vehicle that you occupy at the time of collision—if you are riding with a friend in his or her vehicle, you can collect from your friend's policy and your own policy.
- A family member's policy will provide coverage under that family member's separate policy if the vehicle you occupy at the time of the accident is not owned by any family member or furnished for any family member's use. "Family member" is defined as any person who lives with you at the time of the accident and is related to you by blood, marriage, or adoption, and this includes a ward or foster child.

If you incur medical expenses following an accident, always look to all available sources for medpay even if the accident is your fault.

Medical Payments Coverage Exclusions

Under the standard auto policy in North Carolina, an insurance carrier that provides medpay can limit the coverage by looking to the exclusions under the medpay policy. The following common exclusions limit medpay benefits. The insurer is not required to pay medpay for any injury:

- sustained while occupying the covered auto while it is being used as a delivery vehicle or taxi (this exclusion does not apply to carpools)
- sustained while occupying any vehicle that is being used as a residence
- occurring while the injury victim was engaged in the business of selling, repairing, servicing, storing, or parking vehicles (this exclusion applies only if workers' compensation is available to fund medical expenses for the crash victims)
- for injuries to victims other than the named insured and family members when riding in a taxi or other nonowned auto used to carry persons or property for a fee
- sustained while occupying any motorized vehicle having fewer than four wheels—While we have seen medpay on motorcycle policies in very rare instances, the sole source of medpay for a motorcycle rider would be the single policy covering that motorcycle only if the insurance carrier collected a premium and provided medpay for that specific two or three-wheeled motorcycle.

> ### *Example: Triple Payment of Medical Bills*
>
> Andy is riding with his friend John when Alice runs a red light and collides with their vehicle. Andy incurs $30,000.00 in medical expenses due to the accident. Andy has a private health insurance policy that he pays for himself that pays his medical expenses directly. This type of health insurance has no right of reimbursement in North Carolina. Other than small copays, Andy's $30,000.00 in medical bills are paid entirely by health insurance. John's car insurance provides $5,000.00 in medpay coverage. Andy has his own policy with $25,000.00 in medpay coverage. Even though medical bills were already paid by health insurance, Andy can collect $5,000.00 from John's medpay policy and $25,000.00 from his own policy. These funds are his to keep. Andy can then present his claims against Alice (and her liability insurers) for personal injury and collect medical expenses, lost wages, and pain and suffering. Here, Andy collects another $30,000.00 for his medical expenses plus Alice's insurer must also pay for Andy's lost wages and pain and suffering.
>
> Notice that Andy collects three times for his medical bills! He received $30,000.00 from medpay and $30,000.00 from Alice after his medical expenses were paid in full by his health insurance carrier. While statutory changes have limited the triple recoveries, there are still cases where triple recovery can occur and double recovery of medical expenses remains quite common.

Personal Injury Protection (PIP)

Some states' insurance laws follow a no-fault scheme to provide benefits. In these states, PIP coverage behaves exactly like medical payments coverage. PIP is not underwritten on North Carolina policies. However, if you recently relocated from a no-fault state, your policy may have PIP. Also, if you were riding with an out-of-state guest who has PIP, this coverage would provide another payment source for your medical expenses. Some states' PIP policies also provide benefits for lost income.

Some PIP policies do have subrogation rights. Unlike medpay coverage, the PIP policy may be reimbursed when you collect for your medical expenses through your claims against the at-fault driver's liability insurance.

Rental Reimbursement Coverage

This is an optional addendum available on North Carolina policies. If another driver causes your accident, you should impose the cost of a rental vehicle on the at-fault driver's liability policy. If fault is not yet determined, or if the collision was your fault, your rental reimbursement coverage will pay either $15.00 per day or $30.00 per day depending on the coverage you selected. If you do receive a rental under this portion of your policy, your collision coverage should apply to the rental vehicle so you would not be required to pay the additional cost of a collision damage waiver to the rental car company.

Accidental Death and Dismemberment

This is a rather rare addendum to North Carolina auto policies. If you have this coverage, you can collect stated amounts of cash benefits for certain types of specified injuries and in cases of fatal injury.

Money from Sources Other than Auto Insurance

Commercial/Business Insurance Policies

If a driver is engaged in business when a collision occurs, his or her employer is jointly liable for the victims' claims and losses. Examples include salespeople or executives heading to appointments, delivery drivers, electricians, plumbers, and employees of any other company that requires their employees to leave their headquarters to meet customer needs. Most businesses that have drivers on the road handling their affairs will carry a separate business liability policy that provides additional funds beyond the car insurance available. In some cases, the business policy will be attached to a"fleet policy." Here, all of the business's coverages, including auto coverage and excess business liability coverage, are provided under the same policy.

If you suffer serious or catastrophic injury due to a car accident, always check to see if the driver was engaged in business for an outside employer. This may allow claims against a much larger policy to ensure that all of your losses and claims are honored and paid in full. Most commercial policies carry high limits. We often see $100,000.00 per accident for very small businesses and $1,000,000.00 or more for most businesses.

Please be aware that in commercial insurance cases with serious injuries and high coverage limits, insurers always put the very best adjusters to work defending victim claims. Insurance adjusters are cost-control experts, and they will only focus on minimizing their total claims payment responsibility. It is best to avoid early discussions with adjusters because the laws and evidence requirements are more complex. You truly should have experienced legal counsel speak for you in these cases.

In most cases the business/commercial nature of the at-fault vehicle will be obvious. For example, for a pest-control employee or a florist, the vehicle will have signs identifying the company and advertising their services. However, it is often difficult to discern whether the at-fault driver was on the job when the accident occurred. If your injuries are significant, you can either request an affidavit from the at-fault driver identifying employers and the nature of his or her journey, or compel this disclosure by filing suit and serving interrogatories on the defendant driver. Once suit is filed, you can also compel disclosure and production of the business's driver training standards, driver safety guidelines, vehicle maintenance records, and the employer's full commercial insurance policy.

Because commercial insurance policies carry very high coverage limits, it is imperative that you prepare the most thorough medical evidence in these cases. Unimpeachable medical testimony showing permanency of injury and your expected prognosis will allow you to collect for all future medical care costs and obtain fair compensation for all pain and suffering you can expect to endure over the balance of your life.

Example: Business Policy Pays Million-Dollar Settlement

Our client, Robert O., was injured in a motorcycle accident caused when a driver pulled across his lane to check a mailbox. The mailbox belonged to an auto-body repair facility, and we confirmed that the driver who crossed into Robert's lane was checking for business mail. Since the driver was on a business errand, we were able to reach beyond the car insurance policy and access the body shop's commercial insurance policy. Because Robert's injuries were significant, and because their coverage limits were high, they fought us every step of the way. From the outset the commercial insurer alleged that Robert was speeding, and they denied liability and refused all payment requests. We filed suit and pushed forward toward trial, and we ultimately collected $1,000,000.00 for Robert through a private, out-of-court settlement. We were also able to collect additional money for Robert through workers' compensation because he was a motorcycle mechanic and he was on the job when the accident occurred.

Tractor-Trailer Insurance Policies

If you are involved in a collision caused by a commercial truck, the insurance coverage will be entirely different from a typical auto policy. The laws that govern determination of fault and legal liability are also different.

Truck drivers who operate commercial vehicles across state lines are governed by the United States Department of Transportation. The Federal Motor Carrier Safety Administration (FMCSA) was created to oversee trucking safety due to the dangers involved. Truck drivers face increased safety regulations and stricter laws. For example, they are legally not allowed to text or use cell phones, their hours on the road are strictly limited (to avoid driver fatigue), they cannot be driving while impaired even if their BAC is merely .01 percent, and they are also subject to a large body of law that imposes equipment safety standards on truck drivers and on the trucking companies that employ them.

Truck accident law is quite complex, and accident victims in these cases should always have legal counsel. Truckers are required under Federal motor carrier safety regulations to carry at least $750,000.00 in liability coverage. In some cases, the trucking company will be "self-insured," meaning that they have posted a bond and established proof that they are financially able to pay for accident claims as they arise.

With so much money at stake, trucking companies and their insurance carriers always seek to blame the other drivers involved in any accident. They are slow to accept fault, thus it is often best to use collision coverage to pay for your vehicle repairs to avoid direct dealings with their adjuster. For more information about North Carolina truck accident law, see chapter 8 and the discussion of tractor trailer accidents and visit www.carolinatrucklawyer.com.

Homeowner's Insurance—Umbrella Coverage

This is another type of excess liability insurance that is not part of a car insurance package. The policies are often issued by the same insurance company, but they are truly different policies. The homeowner's umbrella is excess coverage that pays over and above the auto liability policy. The liability insurance coverage on the insured driver's auto policy must be fully exhausted before the umbrella coverage can be accessed. The umbrella policy is essentially extra coverage available to pay for damages caused by the homeowner. It only opens and pays benefits in serious injury claims that exceed the value of all available auto liability coverage.

Umbrella policies are wonderful fund sources, and they typically carry $1,000,000.00 in additional benefits to cover victim claims. This coverage is pure excess, meaning that the coverage is not reduced by the amount of the liability payout. The clue that tells us there is likely umbrella coverage is an underlying auto liability insurance policy with coverage limits of

$250,000.00 per victim, $500,000.00 per accident. Umbrella insurance providers typically insist on this higher level of auto liability insurance to keep the umbrella policy affordable. If we see the $250,000.00 per person limit, there is a very strong likelihood that additional umbrella coverage exists.

If the value of your claims exceeds the limit of coverage available on all available auto liability insurance policies, always look for homeowner's coverage for every driver or vehicle owner who can be held legally responsible for your damages. If the opposing parties will not cooperate with full voluntary disclosure of insurance sources, a simple suit filing will allow you to force disclosure through the court's discovery process.

Health Insurance

If you have personal health insurance coverage purchased privately, provided through your employer, or provided through Medicare or Medicaid, you should always use this coverage to pay for medical needs. Health insurance is not fault based. Thus, whether you cause your own accident, suffer an accident caused by another, or simply fall ill and need medical assistance, health insurance pays for your medical care. We often see accident victims resist using their own health insurance when the accident was not their fault. This is a common and significant mistake! Health insurance protects your credit, provides immediate payment for medical needs, opens doors, and increases treatment options, and the use of health insurance will typically increase the net amount you collect from any personal injury settlement or verdict.

The laws governing health insurance carriers' right to share in your settlement and collect reimbursement from your claims against an at-fault driver are constantly changing. Medicare and Medicaid always have a right of reimbursement. Your attorney should be able to significantly discount the health insurance carrier's reimbursement lien by:

- scrutinizing the Medicare or Medicaid lien to ensure that medical charges not related to the accident are removed from the reimbursement lien claim
- timing the settlement and reimbursement properly so that Medicare or Medicaid can be paid early before their lien claim escalates—This converts coverage back to pure and allows you to seek future medical care without having to reimburse the health insurance carrier from *your* settlement proceeds.
- by active and aggressive negotiation with Medicaid and Medicare's legal representatives. All negotiated discounts are paid directly to the accident victim.

If your health insurance is purchased privately in North Carolina and governed purely by North Carolina law, the health insurance carrier will not have a right of reimbursement. In these cases, health insurance pays and you can collect again for those same expenses through medpay *and* through your claims against all liability insurance for all parties who caused your accident. The federal Affordable Care Act will limit these nonsubrogating health insurance policies, such that, after 2015, all health policies will have a right to some share of your injury claim proceeds.

Workers' Compensation

If you are within the scope of employment when a car accident occurs, your employer must provide workers' compensation benefits, which include full payment for all medical care costs, payment for lost income when work is missed for medical reasons, and lump-sum cash payments for permanent injuries. Workers' comp also must pay to retrain you if you are unable to return to your previous line of work, and they also must provide modifications to your home and workplace when required for injury adaptation.

If you are eligible for workers' compensation and the accident was not your fault, you are still allowed to present your personal injury claims against all at-fault drivers, their employers, and other responsible parties and insurance carriers. The workers' compensation insurance carrier does have a right of reimbursement from your personal injury settlement/ verdict. This amount can be negotiated down privately, and you also have the right to have the workers' comp reimbursement lien claim discounted or waived through legal proceedings filed in the North Carolina state court system. Here, the judge determines the amount that the workers' comp carrier receives from your injury claim proceeds.

Employer-Provided Sick/Vacation Pay

If an accident victim has accrued vacation, sick, or personal leave that he or she can utilize following an accident to avoid paycheck interruption, this is a separate source of collection in the personal injury case. Under North Carolina evidence law, the collateral source rule prohibits introduction of trial evidence that reveals that the victim was able to collect for losses from an outside source. This rule applies to sick or vacation pay. Thus, even if you are paid during your period of medically ordered disability, you can still collect for those lost wages from the responsible driver and his or her insurance carriers. While some disagree with the propriety of this double recovery, it truly is the just result. If you use all of your vacation leave due to an accident, the responsible driver certainly should restore those wages so you can enjoy vacation time later and draw pay from your settlement proceeds.

Short-Term and Long-Term Disability Policies

Short-term disability ("STD") and long-term disability ("LTD") policies provide income benefits if you miss work for medical reasons. These policies can be purchased by private individuals or provided by an employer. In some cases, the STD/LTD insurance company has a right to be paid back for income benefits paid if the collision was not your fault and you are able to collect lost wages from the at-fault driver. In some cases, the income that you received through STD/LTD is not taxable.

Aflac and Other Accident-Triggered Policies

Aflac and similar insurance policies provide cash benefits for specified types of diagnosed injuries and medical conditions. These policies do not have a right to reimbursement and make no claims against your personal injury case proceeds. To trigger this coverage, you typically only need medical records confirming a diagnosed illness or condition that fits the list of covered events on the policy. In most cases, you then receive a single lump-sum payment in the amount specified in your policy.

Crime Victims Compensation Fund

This statutory remedy creates a $30,000.00 account available to pay victims of criminal misconduct who are not paid fully through other sources. While a typical auto accident arising from a simple traffic violation will not be sufficient "criminal" conduct to trigger coverage, DWI is specifically listed as sufficient criminal conduct to allow payment. Accidents caused during auto theft or another criminal enterprise would also be covered.

This fund is a safeguard available only to victims who are not paid through other sources. Thus, the fund is considered a "payer of last resort." To apply and collect, you must show that you are an innocent victim of criminal conduct, that you have exhausted all liability insurance and other payment options, and that these other payment sources were not sufficient to pay your medical bills and other expenses arising from the accident. For example, if you have $75,000.00 in medical bills but the at-fault, impaired driver only has $30,000.00 in available liability coverage, settlement would not pay the full amount of your bills. Application to the crime victims' compensation fund would allow you to collect up to $30,000.00, which would be paid directly to your unpaid medical providers.

For the complete text of the statute with all rules and guidelines, see the North Carolina Crime Victim's Compensation Act at N.C.G.S. Chapter 15B.

Federal Funds—US Agent Causes Accident

The post office is perhaps the most obvious example of the United States government operating federally owned vehicles to conduct official business. Other examples include military drivers, FBI and federal agents, and workers representing the US Department of Transportation.

Before 1946, the US government was immune from suit and civil claims through the doctrine of "sovereign immunity." Thus, if an agent of the government caused an accident, the victim was barred from bringing any claims. This law was changed through enactment of the Federal Tort Claims Act. The federal statutes that embody the act are 28 U.S.C. 1346(b), 28 U.S.C. 1402(b), 28 U.S.C. 2401(b), 28 U.S.C. 2402, and 28 U.S.C. 2671–2680. The various departments and agencies of the government will also have their own regulations that impose notice requirements and rules that must be followed to collect from any employee or agency of that department.

The FTCA provides a remedy and source of federal money for parties injured by government employee negligence. The liability (blame and responsibility for the accident) of the federal agent is determined by state law. We look to North Carolina traffic laws and other state laws to determine whether the victim can collect for injuries and property loss from the federal government. Thus, while the procedural rules change in FTCA cases, all of the advice in this book concerning how to prove fault and how to collect for all damages apply in these cases.

Strict notice requirements apply. Failure to provide a proper and timely notice to the appropriate federal agency bars all claims. Also, in most cases, there is a single-claim limit, meaning that property loss and injury claims must be presented together. For example, if the US Post Office pays for your vehicle damage, they will close the file and legally refuse later payment of your injury claims.

Attorneys' fees are limited to 20 percent of the settlement and 25 percent if a hearing or trial is required to secure judgment. Victims in these cases should always have representation due to the limited fee structure and the complexity of these cases. Attorneys who overcharge victims of accidents caused by federal agents are subject to criminal prosecution!

Prejudgment interest and punitive damages are precluded under the FTCA. Also, if a trial is necessary, the forum is limited to a non-jury trial before a US District Court judge pursuant to 28 U.S.C. 2402. Before filing suit in US District Court, the claimant must first provide notice to the responsible agency and must present the complete statement of the claim for damages to the responsible agency for adjudication.

The FTCA statute of limitations requires the full claim be presented to the appropriate government agency within two years of accrual. The claimant must file a federal court complaint within six months of the agency's denial of the administrative claim or anytime six months after presenting the claim if there is no responsive action or reply from the agency.

State Funds—NC Employee Causes Accident

State governments were also previously immune from lawsuits and civil liability. The North Carolina Tort Claims Act (NCTCA) changed this and allows victims of accidents caused by the negligence of a state employee to collect for the damages and losses. The full text of the statute can be found at N.C.G.S. 143–291 et seq.

The NCTCA designates the NC Industrial Commission (the hearing forum that primarily considers workers' compensation claims) as the court to hear and decide negligence claims against the state and its agents/ employees. While this provides a different setting for hearings/trials of injury and accident cases against state agencies and employees, the law of damages and the rights of compensation are the same as we see in typical accidents involving private parties.

If your accident is caused by a county, city, or municipal employee, sovereign immunity remains and the victim has no legal right of payment from the local government. While the local government may elect to honor certain claims or expenses, this is their choice and they only pay what their internal policies require. They also may choose to deny payment on all accident claims.

In city/county/municipality cases, there are three ways to collect for your losses. First, if a city or county purchases liability insurance to protect them from suit, immunity is waived to the extent of the available coverage limits. Thus, if there is insurance, you can collect exclusively from that source. Second, if there is no liability insurance, the government may still choose to pay certain expenses, even though they remain immune from liability. Third, if immunity remains as a defense, you can use your uninsured motorist coverage as a last-resort payment source for all damages that the municipality will not voluntarily pay.

Example: Winston Salem Fire-Truck Driver Not Liable

An unfortunate example of local government immunity occurred when a Winston Salem firefighter ran a red light while en route to a fire call and caused a devastating car crash. The young woman involved in the collision was hospitalized for her injuries, but she did recover. The city did not purchase liability insurance coverage, and, thus, they had no obligation to pay anything to the victim. City ordinances and policy provided that Winston Salem local funds would only pay for car damage and medical expenses arising from this accident. Nothing more could be collected. Fortunately, our client had a large personal auto policy and we were able to collect all of the remaining damages due by leveling unpaid claims against the UM/UIM coverage on the victim's auto policy.

Personal Wealth and Assets of Responsible Parties

In cases of serious catastrophic injury, we often see auto insurance coverage limits impose a barrier in the amount we are able to collect and recover. In all cases involving serious or permanent injury, the victim or his or her attorney should perform careful asset searches based on public record. One Canadian asset search vendor will actually provide current bank account balances along with a detailed summary of all corporate affiliations, real estate owned, registered owned vehicles, and all other indicia of owned assets and wealth. Also, www.lexis.com has powerful asset search tools that help to locate property and identify wealth and assets.

If the injury claim value exceeds the amount of available coverage, a trial verdict would be necessary to levy against bank accounts and personal property and to perfect a judgment lien against owned real estate. Thus, you cannot collect from the at-fault driver's assets unless you complete a trial. This means you cannot accept the liability policy limits unless you either first prevail at trial or unless you forfeit your right to a trial and give up any claims that exceed the available insurance coverage limits.

In catastrophic injury matters, asset searches should be performed soon after the collision occurs. Unfortunately, we often see responsible drivers facing significant legal liability transferring assets after an accident to divest themselves and avoid judgment. North Carolina law prohibits "fraudulent conveyance" intended solely to avoid creditor claims. Early asset searches paired with subsequent asset searches clearly show wealth transfers made solely to avoid victim claims. These transfers can be halted and reversed by the court.

A large verdict and judgment will occasionally render a responsible driver insolvent. In these cases, he or she may file bankruptcy to avoid payment of the victim's claims. Victim claims arising from a collision caused by a drunk driver are not subject to discharge in bankruptcy. Also, in many Chapter 7 and Chapter 13 filings, the victim can collect some fraction of their judgment from the insolvent debtor's bankruptcy estate.

In the next chapter, we discuss how to choose an insurance company and how to read and understand your car insurance policy. Thereafter, we thoroughly explore how to protect your legal rights after an accident, how to safely report all insurance claims, and how to collect maximum payment for all property damage and injury claims. We review the terms of a proper settlement and consider the steps involved in litigation and trial if the insurance carriers refuse to offer an acceptable settlement for all accident claims.

CHAPTER 2

❖

BUYING AUTO INSURANCE AND UNDERSTANDING YOUR POLICY CONTRACT

In this chapter we discuss how to find the right insurance company, and how to find the best price on quality coverage. We then look at the basic provisions of the North Carolina standard auto policy. At this point, we consider a broad overview of the contents of your policy. Coverage limit recommendations and a detailed description of how each type of coverage applies to pay benefits are discussed in chapter 1.

Buying Auto Insurance

How to Find the Best Insurance Company

Choosing an insurance carrier is both a personal and a business decision. If you have a relationship with an insurance agent and prefer to have him or her underwrite your coverage, this is certainly acceptable. However, the better approach is to look solely at quality of coverage and price. To avoid any negative reaction from individual insurance carriers, we do not recommend certain carriers or identify the more difficult insurers. However, you should be aware that there are a few insurance companies that lead the way in unfair and bullying claims practices.

If an accident does occur, you certainly want to be treated with respect. *All* insurance companies seek to minimize claim payments. While they are legally compelled to pay fairly for vehicle damage and property loss, they never open with generous offers in personal injury cases. However, there are some companies that go beyond aggressive negotiations and continuously overreach in their efforts to underpay claims. These are the companies you want to avoid.

As you set out to buy auto insurance, you should isolate two or three carriers that are price acceptable and then take a few minutes to search the Internet for reviews and evaluations of the claims-handling procedures for each. If you cause an accident, you certainly do not want your insurance company to bully the victims and motivate them to file a public lawsuit against you. On the other hand, if you are struck by an uninsured driver and must present your injury claims against your own insurance carrier through an uninsured motorist claim, you certainly want them to treat you fairly when you seek to collect benefits. Once you locate a number of insurance companies that handle claims fairly, price should be the deciding factor.

Finding Coverage at the Best Price

Several insurance carriers lead their marketing messages with best-price claims. As long as your insurance carrier has a reputation for fair claims handling, finding the lowest premiums should be your only concern. Most insurance companies make their primary profit through investing. They typically make very little in actual underwriting profit on car insurance policies. Today, price competition has brought the profit margins very low.

To find the best price, conduct online searches and also use some of the call-in telephone agencies to compare carriers' prices. Insurance companies have made it very simple to see their exact price for insurance coverage. As you conduct your search, make sure you are comparing the same coverage limits on all available coverages. This will confirm that the lowest price found is indeed the best price.

Contents of the North Carolina Auto Policy

When you first buy auto insurance, the insurance company should send you a complete copy of your policy. Your auto insurance policy is a contract made up of several parts, including the application and binder, the policy declarations, the policy jacket, and the endorsements.

Policy Application

The application is your first inquiry and request for coverage with your insurance carrier. You must be entirely honest and forthright in all insurance applications. Under North Carolina law, a *material misrepresentation* in the application allows the insurance carrier to cancel the policy retroactively and avoid coverage. Thus, if a material misrepresentation in the application is revealed after an accident occurs, you could be left holding the bag on all victim claims and for your own injuries and vehicle damage.

A "material misrepresentation" is the misstatement of any fact on the application, which, if provided truthfully, would have affected the rates/premiums. Many variables can affect premiums. Thus, please always disclose all information fully and honestly when applying for insurance. Otherwise, the coverage you pay for could vanish after an accident occurs.

Coverage Binder

If you do not purchase insurance directly from the insurance carrier, you will be working with an independent agent. Agencies are great to deal with, as they can provide price quotes for multiple carriers simultaneously. Even if the agent is not a direct employee of the insurance carrier, he or she can still place coverage. In these cases, the agency can *bind* the insurance carrier to the obligation to provide insurance. Since a policy has not yet been written, the interim policy document is called a binder. A valid binder is the same as a valid existing auto policy.

Policy Declarations

The "policy declarations" or "declarations page" is the front page of a full auto policy. This is the easiest place to review all coverage choices and premiums. Your policy declarations will provide a quick snapshot of the following information:

- name of insured driver(s)
- address where policy is issued and the principle address where insured vehicles are garaged
- identification of every individual vehicle insured on the policy
- for each insured vehicle, identification of which coverages were purchased and the total coverage limits available for each accident
- list of all endorsements that add unique coverages to your policy or that modify the policy jacket to meet recent changes in law.

Your policy declarations page is the very best way to identify payment sources available after an accident.

Policy Jacket

The policy jacket is a bound booklet that contains the complete North Carolina form auto policy. Our insurance commissioner considers all policy language and approves the forms that can be utilized. Thus, the policy jackets for all auto policies sold by all insurance carriers are identical. While they may vary slightly in look and feel, the language describing and limiting all coverage types is the same. The North Carolina Department of Insurance provides a full copy of the standard auto policy and an excellent consumer's guide to the current North Carolina auto policy at www.ncdoi.com.

Endorsements/Addendums

Endorsements are typically found behind the policy jacket, and they contain additions and revisions to the policy jacket. Insurance laws often change in North Carolina. Further, the insurance commissioner's office frequently passes regulations governing insurance coverage options. Endorsements will identify modifications to the policy jacket that bring your policy into compliance with current North Carolina insurance law.

Addendums are another type of endorsement, and they typically provide optional types of coverage that are described within the standard policy jacket. For example, towing and labor, accidental death and dismemberment, and rental reimbursement coverages are typically identified and described in the endorsements to your policy.

How to Read Your Auto Insurance Policy

An insurance policy is a contract. Thus, disputes over the meaning of language and the validity of a claim for benefits require consideration of applicable contract law.

For purposes of clarity, insurance carriers and the insurance commissioner's office have worked toward a uniform approach that you must follow when reading your insurance policy. Here, we are discussing the four main coverages that are described in the policy jacket (liability, medpay, uninsured/underinsured motorist coverage, and collision coverage).

The definitions are always the starting point as you seek to read and understand your policy. Unless indicated clearly in the policy, all bold terms contained in the policy jacket are defined exactly the way the definition appears at the front of the policy jacket. Therefore, if you are reading a single section to understand a specific coverage type, you must pause at every bold-type term and go back to the definitions at the front of the policy. Read the definition of the term carefully and then apply the full text from the definitions section as though it were inserted in full where the bold-type term appears later in the policy contract.

As you begin reading each coverage section, you will find the *insuring agreement*, which provides a broad statement of all coverage provided under that section. For example, under the liability section of the policy, the insuring agreement will broadly describe everything that the policy may cover after an insured driver causes an accident.

Immediately following the insuring agreement, you will then find the *exclusions*. Exclusions limit the coverage provided by the insuring agreement. To properly understand your policy, consider that the insuring agreement describes everything that might be covered. Thereafter, carefully read each exclusion to see if coverage for your specific occurrence has been carved out and eliminated by the policy exclusions.

Following this approach to reading a policy will allow you to determine whether your insurance should apply to provide benefits to you or another accident victim. Please return to chapter 1 for a careful discussion of what is paid by each coverage type, how to stack multiple policies, how to maximize coverage, and a discussion of all other sources of payment that may assist you following a collision.

Answering Coverage Questions

Insurance adjusters will deny coverage if the accident falls within one of the coverage exclusions in the policy, if the driver of the vehicle was not a permissive user of the vehicle, if the vehicle is not an *insured vehicle* as that term is defined under the policy, or if the accident falls outside the policy coverage period. Whenever a claim denial occurs, the insurance carrier will advise the victim early and should offer a written explanation of the grounds for denial. This denial should be reviewed alongside the full text of the policy to confirm that the denial is appropriate. A coverage denial is different from a liability denial, where the insurance carrier disputes that their insured driver caused the subject collision. In all cases involving coverage disputes, the victim should secure advice and a legal opinion from an experienced insurance coverage lawyer. If there is a valid question concerning application of coverage, a civil action can be filed to put the coverage issue in the court's hands. These actions are called *declaratory judgment actions*; here, the agreed-upon facts are presented to the court, and the court then applies North Carolina insurance and contract law to the facts and the policy language to render a reliable decision on whether coverage should be afforded to cover accident losses.

CHAPTER 3

❖

STEPS TO TAKE AFTER AN ACCIDENT—PLAN OF ACTION, COMMON ACCIDENT CAUSES, APPLY NC TRAFFIC LAWS, CONSIDER HIRING A LAWYER, AND DETERMINE WHO OWES YOU

The choices you make during the first days after an accident are critical. Unfortunately, many victims pause to focus purely on health while insurance adjusters work quickly to establish defenses and find reasons to avoid payment.

In this chapter, we review an accident response plan that will help you to avoid common traps and pitfalls that can threaten your legal rights. We then explore the most common laws that apply in accident cases. Your rights of compensation truly arise from negligence laws and the traffic laws that govern driver conduct. We also consider how an attorney might help you, how to choose and pay for a lawyer, and how you and your lawyer can identify all parties who owe for your accident claims.

What to Do After an Accident

If you are involved in a motor vehicle accident resulting in property damage or injury, you should carefully consider each of the following issues and recommendations:

Take Scene Photos

Whenever possible, parties should secure photographs of the accident scene from various angles to show the condition of the roadway, the position of all vehicles, and the actions of the post-accident response team.

Secure Witness Identification(s)

Independent witnesses can be crucial in the determination of the cause of your car accident. While police reports typically provide accurate information, witnesses who stop to volunteer their time sometimes get away because of slight recording errors. Secure names, all contact numbers, and a permanent address for all witnesses who stop to volunteer their time and testimony. Also, confirm the contact information provided on your police report.

Secure Police Contact Information

Often several officers will assist, leaving just one officer to prepare the official accident report. Law enforcement officers are happy to provide business cards, badge numbers, and contact information. These witnesses can be very helpful during the claims presentation process when you seek to tell your story in full detail.

Secure Vehicle Photographs

If you are unable to take photos at the accident scene, make sure that you secure photographs of the vehicle you were riding in. Photos should be taken from all angles and at several distances. Be sure also to photograph the interior of the vehicle, including the condition of airbags, damage to interior pieces, and vehicle contents. Whenever possible, secure photos of other vehicles involved in the collision. The bottom portion of page 1 of your police report provides information on where all vehicles are towed following a car accident.

Secure Immediate Medical Evaluation

Your health is best served by immediate, thorough medical diagnosis and treatment. Medical records also drive the settlement value of your personal injury case. Please push for a thorough evaluation with a primary-care doctor or specialist and report *every* problem and *every* symptom to your medical providers. Secure all medical treatment recommended, and attend all doctors' appointments. Thorough medical care protects your health. Also, medical records and bills are the insurance companies' primary focus in determining the value of your claim for pain and suffering.

Secure Early and Ongoing Injury Photographs

Visible cuts, bruising, or other serious injuries should be photographed early, and photographs should continue throughout the healing process. This simple evidence is essential following recovery to prove the true extent of injury. Insurance adjusters always try to suggest that the victim is exaggerating injury. Photos answer these doubts every time.

Review Police Reports Early

North Carolina is one of just five states in the United States that follows the pure contributory negligence law. If a victim is slightly at fault for causing his or her own car accident or injuries, he or she has *no* claims arising from the accident. Police report errors can be fatal to your case if they are not corrected early.

Identify All Parties Who Owe for Your Accident Claims

A North Carolina accident victim can collect for injury and accident claims from multiple parties. You must look carefully to identify all errors and dangers that contributed to causing your accident. Refer to the last section of this chapter for a list of parties to consider in every case.

Report Claims to Insurance Carriers

For claims against your own policy, the contract demands that claims be reported in a reasonable period. If you were not at fault, it is common to report claims only to other parties'/drivers' liability policies. However, remember that your own policy may provide overlapping benefits (e.g., medpay coverage pays for medical bills, which are paid again by liability insurance). Thus, it is best practice to report the accident as soon as possible. When reporting claims to other drivers'/parties' liability insurers, avoid providing recorded testimony, avoid discussions about medical details and past medical history, and focus on property damage, accident facts, and general injury description. Do not admit to speeding or other driving errors. If you intend to hire an attorney, do this quickly and allow your lawyer to handle all claims reporting and insurance communications. See chapter 1 for a list of all potential insurance sources and coverage types so you will know what type of claims you should be reporting.

Do Not Sign Medical Authorizations for Insurance Adjusters

You should not sign a blanket medical authorization for the liability insurance adjuster. Insurance adjusters will not help to build your case. They only seek medical authorizations so they can look into your medical past. Preexisting conditions, prior similar symptoms, and even unrelated private medical issues are commonly used as reasons to deny payment of valid injury claims.

Avoid Providing Written/Recorded Testimony to Insurance Adjusters

Friendly adjusters are typically the most dangerous adjusters. If you are a car accident victim, you must understand that the insurance adjuster's goal is to minimize your injury payments. Insurance companies are forced to pay fairly for vehicle damage. However, they angle toward avoiding fair payment for injuries and medical costs. Adjusters only seek recorded statements to collect proof supporting defenses to your claims. You are not legally required to cooperate with their efforts to oppose your case. If liability/fault is in question, always speak with a lawyer first to secure advice on how to properly provide a statement and how to safely respond to the adjuster's questions. An accident lawyer should be glad to answer these questions through a free consultation, even if you prefer to handle your case without an attorney.

Settle Property Damage Claims without Discussing Your Injuries or Your Medical Care

Accident victims should avoid being pulled into early discussions about their injuries. Your words can be taken out of context, and early discussions are only used to solicit tidbits of information that can later be used against you. Please limit early discussions with insurance adjusters to property damage only. It is entirely safe to handle and resolve property damage claims as soon as possible. Our laws protect your right to early payment for property damage without causing any loss in your right to fair compensation for injury claims.

Keep a Journal

To preserve memories and valuable evidence, keep a diary of all difficulties, missed occasions, injury-related problems, and other notes to document your road to recovery. This record will help you to later convey the complete story of your difficulties and medical experience when you present your injury claim demand. If you hire an attorney, begin the journal with

"Dear Attorney …" This renders your journal a privileged attorney/client communication, which allows the lawyer to use parts of the journal based on the attorney's discretion. The other side cannot force disclosure of the full journal if the document is an attorney/client communication due to attorney/client privilege.

Retain Pharmacy Receipts

Pharmacy receipts are often discarded. While these are small expenses in relation to overall medical bills, these receipts are vital proof. Insurance adjusters often point to a lack of pharmacy receipts to suggest that the patient was not cooperating with doctors' orders or that the pain and symptoms were not sufficient to warrant the medication. Please hold on to your receipts!

Do Not Provide Medical Receipts/Records/Bills to the Adjuster until All Medical Treatment Is Completed

Insurance companies never pay victims' bills as they are incurred. Rather, they make a single, lump-sum settlement payment, which should only occur after all treatment is complete and after your health has improved as much as possible. Insurance adjusters want to see medical bills and records along the way so they can cherry-pick the records for evidence that reduces the value of your car accident claims.

Document Out-of-Pocket Expenses

Medical bills are only part of the injury-claim picture. Document all other expenses, including over-the-counter medications, bandages or medical supplies, money paid to others to help with household needs, mileage for accident-related travel, and any other costs incurred in response to the accident.

Secure Medical Excuse for Lost Work Time

Insurance adjusters always attack wage-loss claims. If you miss work for medical reasons, you are entitled to full payment for all lost wages. Even if your employer does not require a work note, the insurance adjuster will. Thus, advise your doctors of your work duties and ask them to document when you can safely return to work. They are typically happy to provide this. If the doctor provides lifting or duty limitations when you are cleared to return to work, follow all medical restrictions to prevent further injury.

Attend All Scheduled Medical Appointments

Adjusters love to fight injury claims by saying that the patient was uncooperative or that the symptoms were not as significant as the victim claims. By attending all medical appointments, you demonstrate your cooperation with medical advice and you give doctors a full opportunity to provide all treatment that they feel would benefit your recovery.

Use All Personal Health Insurance Coverage to Fund Medical Care

This step is crucial. Whether you have private health insurance, employer-provided health coverage, Medicaid, Medicare, or any other type of health insurance, *always use your personal health insurance to fund all accident-related medical care.* Health insurance protects your credit, opens doors, and helps you to access all treatment necessary to support a full recovery.

Determine Whether Your Health Insurance Carrier Has Claims against Your Settlement

In some cases, health insurance pays for medical care and you collect *again* for the same medical bills in your car accident settlement. Here, you collect twice for medical bills! In other cases, you must reimburse your health insurer when the injury case is resolved. Always determine your health insurer's rights early to avoid legal complications that can jeopardize your settlement and/or your health insurance coverage. If your health insurer shares in your settlement, you or your lawyer should negotiate their claim downward to increase your net share of the injury claim proceeds.

Secure Medical Proof of Injury Permanency and Future Medical Care Costs

Insurance adjusters hope to ignore your future medical needs and your future pain and suffering. Further, they never pay for injury permanency or for future pain and suffering without proper medical evidence. Following release from active medical treatment, a qualified medical expert must render an opinion to show permanency of injury and to prove that you will incur future medical care costs. Proper expert medical evidence vastly increases the settlement value of your injury case. If you have a lawyer, let him or her handle all medical inquiries. Lawyers can help you to secure proper medical narratives without alienating your doctors, and we can focus the medical inquiry to help you and your doctors avoid the need for a jury trial.

Secure Economic Proof of Lost Earning Capacity

Serious injuries can cause dramatic changes in your career path. Insurance companies will not pay for these future income losses without proper evidence. A qualified expert in economics and vocational rehabilitation can document the impact of injury and disability on earning ability. If you cannot earn the same pay because of injuries, the responsible parties should pay for this future income loss. Trial experts can also prove lost work-life expectancy in cases where the effect of an injury will likely require early retirement. This evidence allows you to collect now for these lost years of employment.

Speak with at Least One Accident Attorney as Soon as Possible

Free consultations are always available to accident victims. Even if you intend to handle your accident case alone, without an attorney, you should invest your time to speak with a lawyer about your specific circumstances. Avoid attorneys who will not provide a free consultation without pressure. Also, if you prefer to have representation, it is always best to hire an attorney as soon as possible. Once an attorney is involved, insurance companies are not allowed to contact you, and they must work solely with the lawyer who seeks to build your case and protect your legal rights.

How a Lawyer Might Help

Before we review the laws that apply in accident cases, we first consider whether to hire an attorney to protect your rights. If you handle your claims without counsel, you must understand and apply applicable laws to your unique circumstances. If you hire an attorney, you can safely skip the legal analysis because these matters will be your lawyer's responsibility. If you retain a lawyer, you should focus purely on medical recovery and allow your lawyer to handle all investigative steps, all insurance communications, all medical homework, and every other task necessary to protect your rights and increase case value.

Insurance companies take advantage of superior knowledge and leverage when they deal with unrepresented accident victims. In low-force accidents where there are no injuries, attorneys are typically not involved. In cases involving only slight injury, it is wise to speak with an attorney to understand all rights and options. However, the value of the injury claim may not justify legal representation. That is, if the injuries are slight and treatment is concluded in just a few weeks, the overall case value may not justify hiring an attorney and paying an attorney's fee. In cases involving serious injuries, an attorney can generate much higher injury claim payments. Legal fees in injury cases are based on contingency, which means you pay the lawyer only if and when he or she collects money for you. Your attorney should handle property damage claims for free. The fee on the injury claim is paid at the end of the case. To the extent that the attorney increases settlement offers, he or she pays his or her own fee. Most firms charge a third of the total injury settlement. If the attorney significantly increases case value and the total settlement or trial verdict, the fee is justified by these increased payments. In most serious injury cases, the attorney can generate enough *additional* payment to cover the legal fees and still leave the clients with more money than they would have received if they had handled their claims without counsel.

Attorneys in injury cases should provide complete client service—you work with doctors to recover your health, and the lawyer should handle every other aspect of your case. Avoid attorneys who task you with case assignments. You should not be asked to provide your own medical records and bills. A full-service motor vehicle accident firm should handle all of the following for you:

- find all insurance policies and access multiple sources of payment;
- report your insurance claims and handle all insurance communications;
- handle property damage claims for you for free;
- investigate the accident to collect evidence and prove fault;
- help you understand medical treatment options;
- help you coordinate health insurance filings;
- help you deal with income loss and financial difficulties;
- work with doctors to collect medical records and build medical evidence;
- assemble trial evidence and prepare insurance settlement demands;
- aggressively negotiate on your behalf; and
- compel the insurance adjusters and defense lawyers to pay you the highest possible injury settlement or bring your case to trial whenever necessary.

Find a lawyer with medical expertise! The value of a personal injury case is supported primarily by quality medical evidence. The best injury lawyers have a broad scope of medical experience and knowledge. Your lawyer must understand medicine, human anatomy, and how traumatic injury to one area of the body might affect your overall health throughout the remaining years of your life.

Look for a lawyer who will be respected and feared by the insurance companies. Insurance companies are only looking at their money obligations. Most cases settle, but insurance companies know that a trial lawyer will know the true value of your case and they also know that your lawyer will conduct a winning trial if they fail to pay full-value through a private, out-of-court settlement.

If a lawyer stands with you in settlement negotiations, the adjusters know you are not bluffing when we threaten suit in your case. Thus, the adjusters will respond with higher settlement offers. They know if they don't pay our client fairly, we will win at trial and thus force them to pay your claims in full *plus* pay court costs *plus* pay you 8 percent prejudgment interest on the full amount of your verdict *plus* they must hire and pay for lawyers to defend their insured driver at trial. Simply put, we apply legal and financial leverage and medical expertise to compel a settlement on *your* terms, not the discounted terms that the insurance adjuster will push for.

Choose a lawyer who has a great deal of specific experience dealing with car accident cases. These are unique cases, and general practitioners should be questioned carefully to ensure that they have broad medical knowledge along with detailed knowledge of all laws that apply to civil injury trials and motor vehicle collision cases. Also, look for a successful law practice that has experience working with trial experts and that has the financial resources to hire and pay for experts, such as accident-reconstruction engineers, product-design engineers, vocational-rehabilitation experts, doctors and other medical experts, economists, and other car accident experts who might help to build your evidence to increase settlement value. The quality of your evidence will directly relate to the settlement value of your injury claims.

How the Attorney Is Paid

The legal fee is a contingency fee, which means the lawyer receives no fee unless he or she collects money for you. The fee will be a fixed percentage of the total settlement or trial verdict. Most firms charge one-third of settlement and 40 percent of a trial verdict. The higher percentage in litigation reflects the extensive amount of additional work involved in a full trial. You may seek to negotiate a lower percentage. However, even with the one-third fee, hiring an attorney typically is a win-win proposition for the client and the lawyer.

Personal injury lawyers typically secure higher settlements than accident victims who try to handle their cases alone, without an attorney. To the extent that the lawyer's actions and involvement increase case value, the lawyer pays his or her own fee. In most serious injury cases, the accident victim with a lawyer will receive more net money in hand even after the attorney fee is paid. For example, if the insurance adjuster refuses to pay more than $10,000.00 and you then hire an attorney who secures a $20,000.00 settlement, the one-third fee is justified—the attorney does all the work, and you net $13,333.33 after the attorney fee is paid. The Insurance Research Institute conducted a study on the value of attorney involvement, and they found that injury victims with attorneys collected, on average, three and one half times more than victims who handled their cases alone.

Hiring an attorney does not mean you must go to court. Attorneys always seek to settle injury cases privately. However, the attorney is working to increase the payout for the client. Attorneys increase settlement offers by validating your threat of suit, by knowing the true verdict value of your case, by properly interpreting and presenting your medical evidence, by securing more detailed medical evidence whenever necessary, by avoiding insurance defense tactics and payment avoidance traps, by proving the future effect of injury, by proving and collecting for future medical care costs, by controlling insurance communications, and by fighting with proper evidence to collect for all past and future income loss.

North Carolina lawyers are not allowed to pay expenses associated with litigation. However, most personal injury firms will advance all case costs. This allows the victim's case to be properly developed with no early, up-front costs. For example, if an accident-reconstruction expert must be hired to collect evidence and establish fault, the client is ultimately responsible to pay for the expert's fees. However, accident victims facing serious injuries and time out of work may not have the money to hire these experts. If the evidence increases case value, this early investment is fully justified. If the law firm advances the costs so they can be paid later from the settlement, your rights are protected immediately with no up-front charges.

Lawyers also earn their fee and increase your compensation by protecting your settlement from outside claims. Proper handling of settlement disbursal will make a huge difference in your net recovery. For example, if your health insurance carrier has a right to share in your settlement money, your lawyer should negotiate these claims and make sure they take the smallest possible share. The money your lawyer saves goes directly into your pocket. This applies to private health insurance and also to workers' comp, Medicare, Medicaid, Tricare and military coverage, and health benefits paid through vocational rehabilitation programs. If you have no health insurance and your medical bills are due in full, your lawyer should take time to negotiate doctor bills down so you receive a larger share of the total injury settlement.

Common Accident Causes

The first thing that the insurance adjusters will consider is who caused your accident. If you were an innocent guest passenger, you will not have to worry about fault analysis. If you were one of the drivers, you or your lawyers should look immediately at all drivers' actions to identify all driving errors and accident causes and to eliminate any argument that you may have contributed to causation. Remember, if your own errors contributed just slightly to causing the accident, you have no claims or payment rights in North Carolina!

While not a complete list, the following are the most common causes of car accidents:

- **Failure to Yield**—This is the most common cause of North Carolina car accidents. Drivers often fail to see other cars, pedestrians, or motorcycles, and they turn across the path of an oncoming car or pull out from a side street or driveway directly into the path of an approaching vehicle.

- **Excessive Speed**—This factor can be the sole cause of a car accident or a contributing factor among other causes. Excessive speed can be present even when traveling below the posted speed limit if weather or road conditions render it unsafe to travel at the posted legal speed limit. Insurance adjusters often try to blame the victim and suggest that the innocent driver was traveling at an unsafe speed. Remember, North Carolina law provides that if the victim did *anything* wrong that contributed to causing the accident, the insurance companies owe nothing for your injuries. Avoid admitting to excessive speed, and look out for the insurance adjuster's efforts to blame you for the car accident.

- **Failure to Reduce Speed**—This is the charged traffic law violation when a driver strikes another car from behind. Rear-end collisions are very common and can be caused by failure to reduce speed or also by the sudden merge or sudden stopping of the front vehicle.

- **Impaired Driving**—While less common than other accident types, car accidents caused by drunk drivers frequently occur in North Carolina. North Carolina's punitive damage laws allow the victim to collect additional payment in cases where a driver is highly intoxicated or guilty of multiple DWI offenses in North Carolina.

- **Dangerous Road Conditions**—North Carolina has a variety of road types, from major highways to winding mountain roads. In some rural areas, the roads are poorly maintained, making them more dangerous for drivers. Temporary dangers may be present (such as gravel, debris, oil, slick surface), and there may also be unsafe signage (missing stop signs) and unsafe intersections. In these cases, the NCDOT or other local agencies may also owe for the results of your car accident.

- **Improper Equipment**—This factor may be present on the victim's vehicle or on the other vehicle(s) involved. Mechanical defects, such as unsafe brakes, unsafe tires, improper lighting, defective steering mechanisms, and other vehicle defects can be the cause of an accident. In some cases, we can also collect from the manufacturer of a defective product, opening additional fund sources to pay for your injury claims.

- **Improper Merge and Unsafe Movement**—Another common cause of North Carolina car accidents is failure to maintain lane. When a car occupies the blind spot of another driver's car or truck, often, the driver will merge without warning directly into the occupied lane.

- **Overreaction to Danger**—This is a common cause of car accidents, and insurance companies often try to blame the victim for overreacting to a sudden danger. We can help you to prove that your reaction was entirely reasonable because of the sudden emergency that was created by the at-fault driver.

You or your lawyers should immediately investigate the collision scene, review the police report and all photographs, consider points of impact and extent of damage to all vehicles, and secure driver and witness statements. Look also for hidden defendants. For example, if a driver was working when he or she caused your accident, his or her employer would also owe for your accident claims. Consideration of all accident causes will allow you to properly identify *all* causes of your accident to ensure that you can prove all driver errors and collect the maximum payment from all other drivers and insurance carriers who owe for your injuries and vehicle damage.

Relevant Motor Vehicle Accident Law

The applicable law must be applied to the accident facts to determine your legal rights. Evidence and trial procedure laws will be considered in later chapters. Here, we look at the basis for legal action and the laws that grant victims' rights of compensation following an accident.

North Carolina Negligence Laws

To collect money in a car accident case, you must show that you did nothing wrong and you must also prove that other drivers and parties failed to be careful and thereby caused your accident. To establish fault and legal liability, you must establish evidence that shows negligence of other drivers or parties whose errors caused the subject collision.

North Carolina law allows a victim of another person's careless actions (called *negligence*, or failure to exercise the level of care that a reasonable person would when facing the same circumstances) to collect payment for *all* results of the mistake. However, our law follows the *pure contributory negligence* approach. If the victim of a car accident is just 1 percent at fault for the accident, he or she cannot collect *any* money for injury or property damage. There are three exceptions that allow you to overcome the contributory negligence defense so you can still collect for your car accident claims:

1. Non-causative Negligence—If the car accident victim was somehow careless but the error did not contribute to causing the accident, he or she can still collect for all accident claims. An example would be a driver who was slightly impaired and sitting safely at a red light waiting for the light to change when he or she is struck from behind by a driver who was paying no attention to the road.
2. Gross Negligence—If the other driver is guilty of "gross" or extreme negligence, he or she cannot use the victim's contributory negligence as a defense. Thus, a drunk driver cannot avoid payment obligations by alleging that the victim driver was slightly careless.
3. Last Clear Chance—Car accident lawyers use this defense to save the case when it does appear that the victim made driving errors. This defense allows a negligent driver to collect for all accident claims if the other driver could have seen the victim in his or her

"position of peril" and if the other driver had a clear opportunity (or "last clear chance") to avoid the car accident. We often rely on law enforcement interviews and accident-reconstruction experts to establish this defense.

North Carolina Traffic Laws—Rules of the Road

Beyond basic negligence laws, lawyers also look to North Carolina statutes and traffic laws to build evidence to establish fault and legal liability. The following are the most common traffic laws involved in North Carolina car accident cases:

- *Violation of N.C.G.S. 20-138—Impaired Driving*: A person commits the offense of impaired driving if he or she drives any vehicle while under the influence of an impairing substance or after having consumed sufficient alcohol that he or she has, at any relevant time after the driving, an alcohol concentration of 0.08 or more. For commercial drivers, the legal limit for blood alcohol concentration is .04 percent.
- *Violation of N.C.G.S. 20-140—Reckless Driving*: This statute forbids driving "without due caution and circumspection and at a speed or in a manner so as to endanger or be likely to endanger any person or property."
- *Violation of N.C.G.S. 20-141—Speed Restrictions*: Speed is often a factor in car accidents. This statute requires all drivers to obey all posted limits and prohibits the driver from driving at a speed that is greater than "reasonable and prudent under the conditions then existing." Thus, in rain or heavy traffic, speeding violations can occur even if the other driver is traveling within the posted limit.
- *Violation of N.C.G.S. 20-146—Drive on Right Side of Roadway*: This statute requires drivers to maintain their proper lane of travel, to avoid improper lane mergers, and to remain on the right side of any divided road/highway.

- ***Violation of N.C.G.S. 20-148—Meeting of Vehicles***: This statute requires vehicles approaching in opposite directions to avoid crossing center.

- ***Violation of N.C.G.S. 20-149—Overtaking a Vehicle***: This statute requires a vehicle that is passing another to leave two feet of space while passing and to return to the right side/lane only when there is sufficient room to do so. This statute also requires the vehicle being passed to yield to the passing vehicle and to maintain speed to allow the pass to occur.

- ***Violation of N.C.G.S. 20-150—Limitation on Privilege of Overtaking/Passing***: The passing vehicle can initiate a pass only if the oncoming lane is clear, only when the curve or grade of the road allows visibility five hundred feet ahead, and never at double-yellow centerlines or railway crossings.

- ***Violation of N.C.G.S. 20-151—Driver to Give Way to Overtaking Vehicle***: If a driver is being passed, he or she must not speed up or act in a way to prevent being overtaken.

- ***Violation of N.C.G.S. 20-152—Following Too Closely***: This is the most common cause of rear-end collisions.

- ***Violation of N.C.G.S. 20-153—Turning at Intersections***: This statute requires drivers turning right to remain as close to the right curb as possible and drivers turning left to yield to oncoming traffic and ensure that the turn can be made without interfering with the safe flow of traffic.

- ***Violation of N.C.G.S. 20-154—Signals on Starting, Stopping, or Turning***: This statute requires a vehicle intending to turn to use visible turn signals *and* to maintain the visible signal for two hundred feet prior to the intended maneuver whenever the speed limit is forty-five miles per hour or greater. Cars that stop must have proper brake lights and signals as well.

- ***Violation of N.C.G.S. 20-155—Right of Way***: Drivers turning left must yield and give the right of way to oncoming vehicles and to pedestrians in crosswalks. Drivers entering from a driveway, parking area, alley, or side street must yield before entering the adjacent roadway. If two vehicles approach an intersection from different roads at the same time, the driver to the left must yield to the driver to the right.

- *Violation of N.C.G.S. 20-158—Vehicle Control Signs or Signals*: If the other driver disobeyed any signs, painted lines, or traffic controls during the approach to your accident site, this statute provides the basis of legal liability.
- *Violation of N.C.G.S. 20-161—Stopping on Highway Prohibited*: This statute coupled with federal regulations prohibit stopping on the roadway and require disabled vehicles to be moved (when possible) or clearly identified with flares, reflective triangles, etc.

Federal Law—Commercial Vehicle Accidents

If your accident involved a tractor-trailer or other commercial vehicle, you must also review and apply all additional state laws that govern commercial drivers, all training materials for commercial driver's license testing, and all federal law imposed by the Federal Motor Carrier Safety Regulations.

Commercial drivers who never leave the state are not subject to the federal regulations. However, if the driver carries a commercial driver's license (CDL), which would be indicated on your police report, he or she will be subject to stricter laws governing vehicle equipment and safety standards and driver conduct. These laws impose higher standards of care on commercial drivers and on the businesses that own and operate commercial vehicles.

If your accident involved a motor carrier or long-haul truck driver, he or she will be subject to all state laws and also to the strict rules imposed by the Federal Motor Carrier Safety Regulations. These federal laws are extremely complex. Careful application of these rules can help you to bring in hidden defendants and help you show all of the legal violations that led to your collision. Legal duties imposed by the FMCSRs govern driver training, driver qualification, truck equipment standards, truck maintenance and inspection standards, driver hours-in-service limits to avoid fatigue, proper loading of large trucks, cell phone prohibitions, stricter DWI standards, inclement weather driving prohibition, and more strict traffic laws that must be followed by commercial drivers.

For a list of the most common federal regulations involved in truck and commercial vehicle accident cases, see chapter 8 and the discussion of the unique aspects involved in handling tractor-trailer and commercial truck collision cases.

Determine Who Owes for Your Accident Claims

Make sure everyone who owes for your car accident claims is brought in to participate in payment. In serious injury cases, you must always look behind the scenes to make sure that all parties who contributed slightly to causing the accident are involved in contributing toward your losses. You then must unravel all layers of insurance coverage that should apply to provide payment of your claims. Insurance coverage types and money sources are listed in chapter 1. Before you look for insurance sources, you must first identify those who contributed to causing the accident. The following at-fault parties should be considered in every case:

- **All Drivers Involved in the Accident**—This would include drivers of noncontact vehicles if they contributed to causing the collision. If two or more drivers both committed errors, they can be held jointly liable. Further, both of their insurance carriers would be required to open their coverage and participate in claims payment.
- **Vehicle Owners**—North Carolina law provides a "family purpose" doctrine that says that if the car owner provides the vehicle for the general use and enjoyment of the family, he or she is liable just as though the driver was an employee of the owner. Similarly, if the owner of a vehicle is negligent in entrusting the use of the car to the driver, this allows you to reach the insurance coverage and assets of the owner as well.
- **Bar Owners and Providers of Alcohol**—If the accident is caused by a drunk driver, North Carolina law allows you to reach the

servers, vendors, pubs, and restaurants who served the alcohol if you can show that they knew or should have known that the person drinking would take the wheel while intoxicated.

- **Principals and Employers**—If the at-fault driver(s) was working at the time of the accident and if his or her journey was in the "scope of employment," then the company that employs the driver is also fully liable and legally responsible to pay for your accident claims.

- **Negligent Medical Providers**—Under North Carolina law, medical errors are the foreseeable result of the need for medical care. If your injuries and condition are worsened because of medical errors, the original driver owes for these complications. However, in some cases, it is necessary to bring the doctors or medical facilities into the case if medical malpractice results in a significant worsening of the victim's condition.

- **NC Department of Transportation and Road Managers**—If an intersection is dangerous or defective or if the road is poorly maintained and dangerous, state or municipal agencies may be brought into the victim's personal injury case.

- **Vehicle Maintenance Personnel**—If the accident results from negligent maintenance of the motorcycle or the other vehicles involved, we can identify and bring in the parties who failed to use due and proper care to identify and correct mechanical defects.

- **Product and Vehicle Manufacturers**—If the accident is caused or worsened by a defective vehicle component (e.g., faulty tires, brakes), the manufacturer and sellers of the product can be joined as defendants and compelled to contribute toward payment of injury claims.

North Carolina follows the law of joint and several liability. This allows an innocent victim to collect for his or her losses from every person or business that contributed to causing the accident. In serious and permanent injury cases, identifying all parties and all layers of insurance coverage is essential to allow you to collect full compensation for all past and future medical care costs, for all lost income, and for all of the physical pain and emotional suffering arising from your accident.

CHAPTER 4

❖

VEHICLE AND PERSONAL PROPERTY DAMAGE CLAIMS

Property damage claims are typically the first claims to be handled by the insurance carrier. While property loss is far less important than personal injury, the two claims are treated as two entirely separate types of claims in North Carolina. Thus, it is safe to handle property damage claims and be paid in full for all property loss immediately after the accident, and accepting property damage payment will not harm your right to be paid later for personal injury.

Lawyers Are Typically Not Necessary

If you have questions regarding specific property damage issues, personal injury attorneys should be happy to answer these questions through a free legal consultation. If you were injured and do hire a lawyer, your lawyer should gladly assist you with property damage claims with no legal fee for this service. Since the lawyer's involvement typically would not increase the property damage payment, it simply doesn't make sense to pay a lawyer any fee to help. If your injury lawyer does seek a fee for property damage, you should handle this portion of your case independently and without counsel. Frankly, a full-service personal injury lawyer should always stand ready to help you with no charge if this is your preference.

Property damage claims are relatively simple, and insurance companies have virtually no wiggle room to avoid payment. Our former insurance commissioner, Jim Long, and his staff worked hard to establish rules and guidelines that compel insurers to pay fairly for vehicle repairs and total loss claims. Simply put, you can expect the adjuster to provide full and fair payment on property damage claims. This is because our law now forces them to make fair payment. If property damage adjusters could underpay you, they would. Please understand that the adjuster's open and fair dealings in the property damage claims do not mean that you will be treated fairly in the injury arena. The opposite is true. Injury adjusters have discretion and latitude to avoid payment, and they will not help you build your injury evidence or simply volunteer proper payment.

While you may not need a lawyer to handle your property damage claims, it is important to understand what the insurance company truly owes you. This chapter takes you through the property damage claim process in detail, explaining exactly what you are entitled to, what types of claims can be presented, and what type of documentation will be involved in the car repair and total loss claim process.

Property Damage Releases Are Final

Before we consider the details involved in property damage insurance claims, I offer a word of caution about signing property damage releases. Most insurance carriers will pay for personal property damage and vehicle damage claims without asking the victim/claimant to sign a release. A property damage release is a contract where the claimant agrees to accept the proposed payment as full and final payment for *all* property damage claims arising from the subject collision. As long as the terms of the release are limited to property damage only, this type of release will not bar you from later presenting claims for personal injury. However, the property damage release would end any future right to receive additional payment for any other type of property loss claims.

If the insurance carrier asks that you sign a property damage release, you should not execute this document until you are absolutely certain that all property damage claims have been paid, including vehicle damage, damage to clothing and other personal property, injury to pets, financial loss arising from vehicle damage, diminution of value, unpaid towing, and unpaid rental charges. Make sure you have documented all property loss claims, and make sure that all claims are paid in full and to your satisfaction before you sign the release.

Personal Property Loss Other than Vehicle

If the auto accident was your fault, the only claims you can present for damage to personal property would be those specifically covered through the endorsements on your collision policy. In most cases, you will find no such coverage. Homeowner's policies will occasionally provide coverage for damage/loss to expensive personal items. However, most non-vehicle personal property losses are not insured when the owner of the personal property caused the accident.

Innocent drivers and guest passengers can collect for damaged personal property through all liability insurance policies covering the at-fault vehicle and/or the at-fault driver. Typical items damaged include clothing, cell phones, items carried in the trunk or passenger compartment, and other personal items, such as eyeglasses or jewelry.

Non-vehicle personal property claims are paid only at fair market value. This is the value of the item as a used piece of clothing or personal property. Insurers do not owe replacement value. Further, insurers owe the lesser of repair versus replacement. They cannot be compelled to pay for repairs if the fair market value of the item is less than the estimated repair cost. Unfortunately, sentimental value also is not covered. If your personal property is unique or collectible, stand ready to provide thorough proof of full open-market value of the item. For rare items, you should seek the assistance of a professional appraiser who can provide the evidence necessary to secure the full value of items like antiques, jewelry, artwork, and other rarities. The responsible parties and their insurance carriers truly owe every penny your personal property loss is worth.

We occasionally encounter collisions that cause injuries to family pets. In these cases, liability insurers typically will pay all veterinary bills incurred following the accident. Technically, a pet is legally considered an item of "chattel," or personal property. As such, the true legal obligation in fatal pet injury cases is simply to pay the fair market value that the pet would sell for in the pet market. Thus, whether the animal was a rare breed, whether the animal was used for breeding purposes to produce income, and the pet's age and other qualities would be relevant to value determination. Frankly, the law should allow more compensation in these cases. Pet owners should be able to recover for emotional loss when pets are injured, but the law simply treats pet injury as a category of personal property loss.

Auto collisions also commonly cause damage to land and buildings. These items are also covered under the liability insurance policy. Landscaping, trees, and shrubbery are covered at the full, fair cost of labor and materials to repair the damage. The same rule applies for damages to building and structures. Some counties and municipalities will also present claims against the at-fault driver for damage to road signs and traffic controls.

Vehicle Damage Claims

If your vehicle was damaged in an accident, you should maintain control of the damage claim process. Depending on fault, you will first have to choose which insurance company will be handling repair estimates and payment. In this section, we will review coverage options, rental car obligations, allowable use of used or after-market parts, how to control the repair process, what is owed for lost value of your vehicle, how to deal with towing and storage charges, what is owed if your vehicle is a total loss, the effect of vehicle financing on a total loss claim, and how to secure fair payment on all vehicle damage claims.

Source of Coverage—Which Insurer Owes?

If the collision was not your fault and your vehicle is damaged, you have three potential sources of coverage for vehicle repair or replacement:

liability insurance, uninsured motorist coverage, and collision coverage. If the at-fault driver had insurance when the accident occurred, the liability policy covering the vehicle and driver who caused the accident will provide payment for vehicle repair or replacement, towing charges, storage charges, rental car expense, and diminution of value. If the at-fault driver did not have insurance, you turn to your uninsured motorist policy for coverage. This coverage is subject to a $100.00 deductible, which is far less than the typical collision deductible. If the at-fault driver's liability insurance carrier is slow to accept fault or difficult to deal with, you always have the third coverage option, which allows you to collect for vehicle damage claims through your collision policy.

Collision is optional coverage in North Carolina. Thus, to secure payment, you must confirm that there is collision coverage for the vehicle involved. Collision coverage is also subject to a deductible. Your deductible is the uninsured portion of the vehicle damage claim, which you pay first, and then insurance pays all damage claims that exceed the amount of your deductible.

If fault is clear and injuries are relatively minor, you should allow the at-fault driver's liability coverage to pay all vehicle damage claims. However, in cases involving disputed liability or serious injury, you should handle vehicle damage claims under your own collision policy. This allows you to avoid immediate dealings with the liability insurance company that will defend the at-fault driver and oppose your injury claims. In some cases, your collision carrier will even agree to waive the deductible and pay the full cost of repairs/replacement. Even if a deductible applies, this is a small investment to protect your rights and your privacy.

Collision coverage is no-fault coverage. The mere occurrence of a collision resulting in vehicle damage triggers coverage, regardless of who caused the accident. If the accident was not your fault, use of collision coverage would not result in policy cancellation or cause any increase in your premiums. Further, as soon as all vehicle damage claims are paid, your collision insurance carrier will immediately secure reimbursement through a legal claim called *subrogation*. Through this process, your insurance company will approach the at-fault driver's liability insurance carrier on your behalf to recoup their claims payout *and* your deductible.

As a former insurance adjuster, I can assure you that insurance carriers use property damage claims to earn your trust. Don't take the bait. Their hands are legally tied, and they are required to tender fair payment for all property damage claims. While some cases can be difficult, most property damage claims do not involve dispute. Please understand that insurance carriers pay full and fair value for property loss because they are legally required to do so. They then use the process to build trust so they can later control the injury claim. They often also seize the opportunity during property damage dealings to initiate injury discussions to gather evidence that can later be used to diminish or oppose your injury claims. Be very careful in all property damage discussions, and limit those adjuster conversations purely to property loss matters.

If the accident was your fault, collision coverage is the only source of payment for towing, storage, and vehicle repair/replacement cost. If you loaned your vehicle to another friend who caused the accident while driving your vehicle, collision remains the only source of coverage. If you did not purchase this coverage, you have no right to payment for your damaged car.

Repair Versus Total Loss

The first question addressed in your vehicle damage claim is whether the vehicle will be repaired or replaced. A "total loss" occurs when it is less expensive to replace the vehicle than to repair it. Repair costs would include the full cost of all repairs, rental car charges during the course of repairs, and any claim for diminution/loss of fair market value. Total loss / replacement costs would include the fair market value of the vehicle plus the cost of a rental vehicle for a limited period of time. The insurance adjuster who evaluates your vehicle damage will look at the full cost picture, and they legally owe to either repair or replace the vehicle, depending on which is cheaper.

The law forces insurance carriers to handle the claim as a total loss and pay replacement value whenever the estimated cost of all repairs equals or exceeds 75 percent of the fair market value of the vehicle. In these cases, the insurance carrier is legally barred from repairing the vehicle and they must pay the claim as a total loss.

Repair and total loss claims are very different. In the following sections we explore all of the details involved in the insurance claim process for each of these case types.

Vehicle Repair Claims

What Is Owed

If your vehicle is damaged in a collision, the responsible insurance carrier owes the full cost of repairs at a repair shop you choose. They also must cover rental car expense during the course of necessary repairs, tow charges arising from the collision, and payment for diminution of value. We review each of these cost elements in detail.

When determining the cost involved to properly repair your vehicle, most insurance carriers will send their own appraiser to handle the initial damage repair estimate. These estimates can be done at your home, at the tow yard, or at the repair shop. Typically, the initial estimate is not enough to cover all costs of repairs. This is because the first estimate only covers visible surface damage and obvious necessary repairs. Insurance companies are forcing the body shop to identify all hidden damage before they pay. When the repair process begins and the vehicle is dismantled, any underlying additional damage will be claimed directly by the body shop. This is known in the industry as a *supplement*.

Please understand that the body shop *will* push for the full cost of repairs. They make money selling parts and labor service time. They also understand that they are responsible for faulty repairs. Thus, they are motivated to point out all hidden damage to ensure that the repair process is completed perfectly. If they do need additional repair money through a supplement, they will contact the property damage adjuster directly and give the adjuster an opportunity to revisit the shop or otherwise determine the necessity of additional repair costs. The responsible insurance carrier typically makes these additional payments directly to the body shop. Thus, when you pick up your vehicle, your repair invoice will typically exceed the amount of the initial repair estimate.

Allowable Use of Used or Reconditioned Parts

North Carolina law does allow the use of used parts and reconditioned parts in the vehicle repair process. As a practical matter, most repair shops and insurance carriers will not use used or after-market parts when the damaged vehicle is less than two years old. Also, your repair shop will reject used parts or reconditioned parts if they are not in perfect condition. Thus, you really should not fear the use of used parts in the repair process. If you choose to reject used, reconditioned, or after-market parts, you must personally pay for the additional expense involved in the use of new, original-equipment parts.

Choosing a Repair Facility

Accident victims are often steered toward certain body shops and repair facilities. This can occur at the towing stage where the wrecker driver suggests a facility. Shop recommendations also occur in discussions with insurance adjusters. The first thing you should know is that you have the sole right to choose who handles your vehicle repairs.

Many insurance carriers typically work with repair shops with labels, such as "approved," "certified," "blue-ribbon," or other indicia suggesting the insurance carrier promotes the use of the particular dealership or body shop. This approval does not require you to use these facilities. If you have a relationship with a body shop or you prefer to use the manufacturer's dealership facility, this is your legal right. However, it is also safe to work with the insurance company's "approved" shop.

Insurance carriers will only approve of a facility if they have a course and history of honest and successful business dealings with that shop. Further, approved facilities will only employ ICAR certified repair technicians. The ICAR certification is the highest level of body repair training in the industry. Further, if you use the insurance carrier's approved facility, typically, the insurance carrier will extend the body shop's standard repair warranty so that your collision repairs remain warranted for as long as you own the vehicle. With these advantages, it is often wise to allow the approved repair facility to handle your repairs.

Rental Car Versus Loss of Use

The at-fault driver owes the cost of a temporary substitute vehicle provided during the course of your vehicle repairs. The liability insurance company is legally required to begin providing a rental only after they have investigated the collision and determined that their insured driver was solely at fault for the collision. If you need a rental before they have completed the investigation, you can pay for the rental car early and seek reimbursement at a later point. Please be careful to pay only standard insurance rental rates if you personally rent a vehicle expecting reimbursement.

Enterprise Car Rental is the leading provider of insurance rentals in North Carolina. If you work with their office, they can provide you with the daily rate for insurance rentals. If you prefer another rental provider, make sure that they are willing to honor the current insurance industry daily rate. Once fault is accepted, most liability insurance carriers will allow a direct bill rental. Here, the insurance carrier provides the rental vehicle with very little paperwork, and they pay directly so there is no need for you to pay first and await reimbursement.

Collision coverage on your own auto policy will transfer to a rental during periods of breakdown or repair. However, if you do not have collision coverage on your damaged auto, you will have to personally pay for the collision damage waiver (CDW). The CDW covers damage to the rental car during the rental period. Unfortunately, if your car was damaged by another driver, but you did not have collision coverage, you remain personally obligated to pay for the CDW. Under North Carolina law, if you do not have collision coverage at the time of the accident, the law perceives providing a rental car with collision coverage as *betterment*. Therefore, the liability insurance carrier is not legally required to pay for the CDW charges. If you cannot afford the CDW, you should forego the rental car and instead collect cash payment for *loss of use*.

As you consider whether to pay additional daily expenses for the collision damage waiver on the rental car, you should look first to see if you already have this coverage. If your vehicle carried collision coverage at the time of the accident, your collision policy covers the rental car during the period where your vehicle is out of service due to damage and repairs. Thus, you are already insured! Also, many premium credit cards carry CDW coverage when you use that credit card to pay for rental coverage. American Express Gold and several premium Visa and MasterCard accounts provide this benefit. Check with your credit card provider, and if this service is available, you automatically receive CDW coverage with no daily charge whatsoever.

If you prefer not to receive a rental car, you have the option instead to collect for loss of use. A loss of use claim allows you to collect compensation because you are deprived of access and use of your own vehicle. This is a cash payment in lieu of a rental car, and most insurers will pay $15 to $25 per day for loss of use. If you have access to another vehicle and can avoid a rental, this is an excellent way to collect additional money above the total loss payment or vehicle repair cost.

Approving Body Shop Repairs—You Are the Customer

Even though the insurance company pays the repair bill, please remember you are the owner of the vehicle and you indeed are the body shop's customer. You had the ultimate choice of repair facility, so you granted the job to the shop. Thus, you should be happy with all repairs. When your vehicle is ready, take the time to inspect it carefully to make sure that all damages were addressed, paint colors match, all pieces are properly attached, and the vehicle functions exactly as it did before the accident. Body shops typically are happy to allow you a test drive to ensure that the vehicle performs properly. Also, ask for a written copy of the body shop's warranty policy. Repair defects sometimes surface only after the vehicle is driven for a brief time. If problems do appear, immediately notify the body shop and the insurance adjuster. This will document repair defects early and ensure that responsible parties pay any remaining costs necessary to properly complete *all* repairs.

Paying the Shop

In most cases, the insurance adjusters handle the initial estimate and will then send the repair check directly to you. If the vehicle is financed and you collect for repairs under your collision policy, they may list the bank/lien-holder as co-payee on the check. The bank will gladly co-endorse, and this extra step is taken simply to ensure that repairs are completed. You are not able to pocket the repair money and forego repairs because this would deplete the value of the vehicle, which is collateral to support the bank's auto loan.

The repair check will typically be for the amount of the initial estimate. If the body shop finds additional damage, they will notify the insurance adjuster and collect for the additional repairs directly. Thus, even though the repair cost may exceed the amount of the insurance company's repair check, that check will be all you need to pick up your vehicle and pay for all repairs.

The best way to control the insurance payment and approval of the shop's repairs is to hold the insurance check until the vehicle is ready. Do not endorse the check or deposit it. Instead, when repairs are complete and you have inspected your vehicle to confirm that all repairs are proper, you can endorse the insurance check as "payable to" the shop. This approach will help you control repair funds until the vehicle is ready, and the shop will walk you through the simple process.

Diminution of Value

Most used car buyers are concerned about the maintenance and repair history of a used vehicle. If your car is involved in a collision requiring significant repairs, this will reduce the fair market value of the vehicle in a later sale. You can collect for this loss from the at-fault driver's liability insurer.

The diminution of value claim is not as large as most owners expect. Cars can be repaired such that they retain full mechanical integrity. Most vehicles are designed for unibody construction. With this type of design, the body of the car is actually the frame of the vehicle. Further, all manufacturers design these frames with pre-engineered "crumple zones", which are weaker spots in the frame/body. On impact, the car will fold at these points, which increases the extent of crush damage so that the vehicle absorbs impact energy. This reduces impact trauma for occupants and renders these vehicles much safer.

The unibody structure is built with high-strength, low-alloy (HSLA) steel. This type of steel can be bent and returned back to its original shape without losing strength or structural integrity. Simply put, frame damage is common and occurs in almost all collision impacts. It will not affect the function or mechanical integrity of your vehicle, and frame damage can be properly repaired on today's automobiles. However, extensive repairs will affect the resale value of your vehicle.

Diminution of value is typically not covered under the collision policy. Thus, you can only collect this if you are presenting claims against the liability coverage for the at-fault vehicle. With the advent of CARFAX and other online vehicle history database services, it is impossible to hide the history of collision repair. Further, North Carolina law mandates disclosure on the bill of sale whenever a vehicle is sold if the vehicle has had collision damage with repair cost that equals or exceeds 25 percent of the fair-market value of the vehicle. Thus, you must actively inform the used-car buyer of the prior collision.

Diminution of value is difficult to prove with certainty. The goal is to determine how much value the car lost because it has been through a collision. Repairs typically restore all cosmetic damage completely. In some cases, the paint blending process will actually leave your car looking better than it did before the accident. However, a skilled technician will be able to discern that the car has been through the body-repair process. Vehicle history reports would also indicate that the vehicle underwent collision repair. Since this affects value, we must consider how to determine the dollar amount of value reduction.

To begin the process, you should formally request payment for diminution of value from the liability claims adjuster. Simply let them know that, when the repairs are completed, you are asking for payment for diminution of value of your vehicle. Under the North Carolina Administrative Code, you are required to report and present this claim within thirty days of conclusion of repairs (11 N.C.A.C. 4.0421(5)). Once the notice of intent to claim is made, you must allow all repairs to be completed. After the vehicle is repaired, you must make the vehicle available for adjuster inspection. Here, they are looking at the quality of repairs and the condition of your vehicle in relation to the same model vehicle that has not undergone collision repairs. The adjuster will typically photograph the vehicle, and if they do not already have full documentation, they will request a copy of the final repair estimate.

The typical offer for diminution of value is approximately 10 percent of the total cost of repairs. While this would not be appropriate for a unique or collectible vehicle, this range is appropriate in most cases. While vehicles are discounted if they have been through the repair process, used car value is typically not depleted. Further, because the repair process is engineered into most vehicle designs today, proper collision repair should restore the vehicle to perfect cosmetic and mechanical condition. Nevertheless, you certainly should be paid some amount for the loss of value.

To respond to the adjuster's offer, you can also seek your own evidence of diminution of value. Many claimants begin with a statement from the local dealership that sells the same brand of vehicle. The used car manager may be willing to offer a written statement of the amount he or she perceives your vehicle has lost in value. Be aware that most of these estimates are extremely high. They are hoping to secure your business and often use trade-in value in their computations. Trade-in value offered by a dealership is not the appropriate value reference point. Instead, the dealership must provide a statement of what they would be able to sell the vehicle for in a fair, arm's-length transaction to a willing buyer. Unfortunately, if you actually sell your vehicle to determine diminution of value, the responsible insurance carrier will accuse you of dumping the vehicle at below-market price simply to determine the amount of your claim for diminution of value.

The best approach would be to hire an independent appraiser who represents insurance carriers and private vehicle owners. An Internet search for "diminution of value appraiser" should help you to locate an experienced appraiser in your area. The appraisal would be at your expense, but the cost is typically less than $200.00. A qualified appraisal would be admissible trial evidence, and this hard evidence should help you to motivate the adjuster to extend higher offers.

Insurance carriers often refuse to pay any diminution of value if the vehicle is more than five model years old. Other states, such as Georgia, follow this approach by concluding that collision damage is typical wear and tear for a vehicle of this vintage. Also, some insurers refuse to pay diminution of value unless the repair cost equals or exceeds 25 percent of the fair market value. Their reasoning is that, in these more conservative repair cases, North Carolina law does not require disclosure of prior collision repairs on the bill of sale. You can respond by noting that prior collision repairs would be a material part of any used-car transaction and that it would be "fraud in the inducement to contract" to hide the fact of prior repairs. Thus, regardless of the cost of repairs, disclosure remains mandatory in all cases.

Statutory Diminution of Value Claims

There is an alternate method for handling your diminished value claim that became effective on January 1, 2010. Below is an outline of North Carolina General Statute 20-279.21(d)(1), which sets out the new option. If the insurance company has not obtained an appraisal, this approach will compel them to get an appraisal.

Step 1—First, you and the insurance company must be unable to agree on the difference between the fair market value of your auto immediately before your accident and immediately after your accident.

Step 2—The difference between your opinion and the insurance company's opinion of the value of your claim must be greater than the lesser of $2,000.00 or 25 percent of the fair market value (as determined by www.NADA.com) of your car.

Step 3—You must send a written demand to the insurance company to select a competent and disinterested appraiser.

Step 4—Both you and the insurance company must select a competent and disinterested appraiser (you each pay for your own appraiser) within twenty days after your demand, and each of you must notify the other of your selection.

Step 5—The appraisers must independently appraise the loss. If the appraisers disagree on the fair market value of your auto immediately before your accident and immediately after your accident, then the appraisers must select a competent and disinterested third appraiser to serve as an umpire. The cost of the third appraisal will be shared by you and the insurance company.

Step 6—If the appraisers are unable to agree on this third competent and disinterested appraiser, then you or the insurance company may request that a magistrate select the umpire. The deciding magistrate must be a resident in the county where (a) the accident occurred or (b) the insurance company's policyholder's vehicle is registered.

Step 7—The appraisers must submit their appraisals and value evidence to the umpire, and the umpire must prepare a report determining the amount of your loss and provide the report to you and the insurance company. In deciding the loss and preparing the report, the umpire shall make no determination of liability and must award damages that are in between the determinations of the two primary appraisals.

Step 8—You and the insurance company have fifteen days from the filing of the umpire's report to notify the other party of your rejection of the umpire's determination. If you or the insurance company fails to reject the umpire's determination within fifteen days, then the umpire's determination and report are binding upon both you and the insurance company. If a challenge is timely made, the diminution of value claim must be then be litigated to conclusion.

Total Loss Claims

If the insurance adjuster determines that the cost of repair plus rental car expense during repairs plus the likely diminution of value would exceed the simple cost of paying the pre-accident value of your vehicle, they will purchase your vehicle through a forced sale known as a total loss claim. Beyond adjuster discretion, where they compare repair cost versus replacement cost, the law forbids repair and mandates a total loss whenever the estimated repair cost equals or exceeds 75 percent of the pre-accident fair market value of your vehicle.

How Total Loss Value Is Determined

Our insurance commissioner's office (ICO) has historically been very consumer oriented in their oversight and regulation of total loss claims. Many years ago, insurance carriers consistently tried to underpay these claims. They followed a pattern of seeking low cost bids and, after determining value, willfully offering less than true fair market value with an eye toward buying your vehicle at the lowest possible price. This approach is now disallowed under ICO regulations and the North Carolina Administrative Code (NCAC).

Any insurance carrier handling a total loss claim must now complete a thorough, fair market value appraisal of the subject vehicle. This requires the insurance carrier to look beyond value guides, such as the *Kelley Blue Book* and the *National Automobile Dealers Association / NADA Guide*. This value appraisal method is somewhat similar to a real estate appraisal. The adjuster must look into the community's used car market and locate vehicles that are for sale or that have recently sold that are the same year, make, and model as the subject vehicle. They are also looking for the same engine and options package and similar mileage and condition. Identical vehicles are rarely available. Thus, insurance adjusters must make value adjustments to allow for differences between comparable vehicles and the vehicle being appraised.

Essentially, the insurance carrier must do enough homework and collect sufficient evidence of vehicle value to be prepared to attend a trial to prove the true fair market value of your vehicle. Once these steps are undertaken, they are then required to extend the full fair market value in their total loss offer. For this reason, insurance adjusters are typically nonnegotiable in the total loss claim. If they have done proper homework, they should be extending a true fair-value offer and negotiation would not be necessary.

Claimants facing total loss offers typically do not need legal representation. This is because the insurance commissioner's office has taken away the insurance companies' opportunity to undervalue these claims. While insurance adjusters used to commonly underpay total loss claims, the law now forbids this. Please do not credit the insurance company for their fairness. Our insurance commissioner legally forced insurance companies to handle these claims fairly to overcome an established pattern of unfair claims practices in the total loss arena.

Confirming the Adjuster's Total Loss Value

When the insurance adjuster extends an offer on the total loss, you are legally allowed to force them to disclose the sources of their value determination. This disclosure should include the description of your vehicle, a list of all equipment and options, a mileage statement, a list of comparable vehicles, book values, a description of your vehicle's condition, and an explanation of all calculations, deductions, and additions used to arrive at your total loss offer (11 NCAC 04.0418(4)). When reviewing the insurance adjuster's homework, make sure that due consideration was given to your vehicle's condition. If the car was in very poor mechanical or cosmetic condition, you will see deductions. These are appropriate considering the used car value would be lower if the vehicle is not in average condition. If your vehicle was in better-than-average condition prior to the collision, the adjuster is legally required to give due consideration to this fact in determining total loss value (11NCAC 04.0418(1)).

The paperwork you will receive from the adjuster typically will include some reference to *NADA* and/or *Kelley Blue Book* values along with research reflecting the current used-car market for vehicles of the same year, make, and model. Many insurance carriers use database valuation services, such as the Certified Collateral Cooperation (CCC). These companies monitor actual sale prices in the used-car market on a nationwide scale. They are easily able to restrict their value calculations to local market areas. These services are typically very reliable, and they offer value appraisals to insurance carriers and private individuals.

Challenging the Total Loss Offer

Since the insurance carrier is required to secure evidence supporting the value and then extend the full appraised value in their total loss offer, they typically will not negotiate or increase their total loss offer.

The only way to challenge their offer and seek an increase is to impeach the insurance carrier's research. In cases where the vehicle model is very common, insurance adjusters often will not negotiate even if you find errors in their research. However, obvious errors will give grounds for a successful challenge.

Example—Increasing Total Loss Payment

Following a collision, John is advised that his vehicle will be handled as a total loss. After receiving his offer, he realizes that his own research suggests a much higher value. John requests the insurance carrier's evaluation and receives a written report including a list of comparable vehicles that were reportedly sold recently in the community market. The report also included some vehicles that were available for sale. John invested additional time to contact the dealers listed on the report and learned that the prices reflected in the insurance carrier's report were incorrect. He confirmed that certain vehicles on the report were not actually available. He also confirmed that the listed sale price was below the actual sale price. After reporting these errors, John provided his own homework showing vehicles that were actually available. John took the extra and proper step to contact the sellers to negotiate down to actual bottom-line sale price. With this additional homework in hand, John was able to motivate higher offers and resolve his total loss claim.

If your vehicle is rare, vintage, or exotic, you should be much more actively involved in the total loss evaluation process. Rare vehicles like vintage muscle cars or collectibles will not fall into *NADA* or *Kelley Blue Book* guides. Further, comparable vehicles may not be available in your community. In these cases, you should perform careful research on your own to locate auction prices, actual sales of true comparables, and quotes from experienced dealers. Also, it is appropriate to use a nationwide search for comparable vehicles, as these more valuable vehicles are commonly shipped to buyers, and state-to-state sales of high-price vehicles are quite common.

What Is Included in the Total Loss Payment

The insurance adjusters will extend an offer of the value of the vehicle. Once the price is agreed to, they will pay the full amount directly to you if you hold clear title to the vehicle. If financing is involved, the insurer will pay the full principal due on the loan and any remaining amount will be paid directly to the owner. In all total loss payments, the insurer will also extend payment of 3 percent sales tax (which allows you to purchase a used replacement vehicle and pay the attendant tax) and tag and title transfer fees (approximately $45.00).

Effect of Vehicle Lease/Financing

If you own your vehicle outright and personally hold the certificate of title, you will receive the full total loss check at the conclusion of the claim. If the vehicle is leased or financed, the finance company will be first in line for payment. In a leased vehicle case, you simply walk away from the vehicle and the insurance carrier would pay off the full balance due under the lease contract. All leases carry GAP insurance coverage, which protects you if the lease payoff is higher than the total loss value. GAP stands for "guaranteed asset protection." If the lease payoff is $15,000.00 and the total loss payment/value is only $12,000.00, GAP coverage pays the additional $3,000.00 to the bank so that you owe nothing further under the lease contract. Once you learn that your leased vehicle will be handled as a total loss, you can typically begin working immediately with the leasing company to enter a contract to replace the vehicle with a substitute lease.

If your vehicle is financed, significant complications can arise in a total loss claim. Under North Carolina law, financing is not relevant to the determination of value in a total loss case. Longer auto loans that extend five and six years often leave the buyer "upside down" on the financing during the first years of the loan term. Vehicles depreciate quickly with time and use. However, auto loans are amortized over the duration of the loan such that early loan payments are primarily interest payments. Thus, early loan payments do not significantly reduce the principal due on the loan. Unfortunately, if you owe more than the vehicle is worth, the insurance adjuster in a total loss case is not required to pay off your loan. If you do not have GAP insurance coverage on the loan, the total loss payment would be made directly to the financing company to reduce the loan balance. The bank would release the title to the insurance carrier, but they would still be legally allowed to collect the remaining balance (known as a "deficiency balance") directly from you.

GAP insurance coverage is recommended in every vehicle financing contract. GAP insurance covers the situation where the vehicle is stolen or destroyed and the total loss insurance payment is less than the current balance due on the loan. GAP insurance is very inexpensive, typically adding approximately $30.00 or less to the monthly loan payment. In negative equity cases where the buyer owes more than the vehicle is worth, the insurance adjuster pays the total loss value to the finance company and the finance company will collect the remaining balance due directly from the GAP insurance carrier. Here, you walk away from the vehicle transaction. While you do not receive any additional payment, this is appropriate, as you had no equity in the vehicle.

If you do not have GAP coverage and the total loss offer is less than the balance due on your car loan, you can approach the dealership and finance company to work directly with them toward possible solutions. In some cases, the finance company will allow a "collateral swap." This is the bank's option, and you cannot force them to accept a collateral swap. If the bank will agree, they allow you to use the total loss claim proceeds to purchase a replacement vehicle. They then accept the title to the replacement vehicle as substitute collateral for your existing loan. Thus, your payments and loan term remain unchanged. After receiving the new title, the bank will release the title to the damaged vehicle to the insurance company.

If you have manufacturer affiliated financing (e.g., General Motors Acceptance Corporation, American Honda Finance, etc.), you may be able to work with the dealership to confront the deficiency balance situation. In some cases, they will allow you to purchase a new vehicle and fold the unpaid deficiency balance forward into the new loan. If this is allowed, you would have no equity in the replacement vehicle because the new loan includes the purchase price of the new car plus the balance due on the total loss vehicle. However, if you add GAP coverage to the new loan contract, you would be protected in the event of a subsequent collision and total loss.

Towing and Storage Charges

The insurance carrier handling the total loss claim will be responsible for costs of towing your vehicle from the accident scene. If the vehicle is taken to a wrecker yard, the wrecker service is allowed to charge a storage fee for each day that the vehicle remains on their property. Once the adjuster determines your vehicle is a total loss, they will ask for your permission to move the vehicle to a storage free area. You should make sure that all personal belongings are removed from the vehicle immediately and allow the insurance carrier to move the vehicle.

You do not give up rights of possession or ownership by allowing the insurance carrier to move the vehicle. Rather, you are honoring your legal obligation to mitigate damages by cooperating with allowing the vehicle to be placed in an area where daily charges (typically $25.00 per day) are not accruing for unnecessary storage. The insurance carrier must seek your permission before moving the vehicle. The insurance carrier will be responsible for this second tow charge. You may also elect to have the vehicle moved to your property if you prefer. However, this would require a third tow charge, which will be your responsibility if you do not retain the salvage vehicle at the conclusion of the total loss claim.

Rental Car Obligations

North Carolina law is not generous in allowing rental car coverage in total loss claims. If the vehicle is repaired, they must keep you in a rental for the entire duration of the repair process. In a total loss claim, the insurance carrier is only required to keep you in a rental up to the date that they tender an offer on the total loss. *Tender* is a legal term that means make the money available. Common practice is to only allow a rental for three business days after the date that the adjuster verbally conveys an offer by telephone. While some insurance carriers will agree to extend the rental for a longer period of time, they are not legally required to do so. If you had to wait for a rental at the beginning of the claim, you may be able to seek the additional days of rental car payment at the end of the total loss process.

As soon as you learn that your vehicle will be handled as a total loss, you should immediately begin looking for another vehicle. Also, if you are able to borrow or use another vehicle in your household, you can forego the rental vehicle and instead collect a cash payment for loss of use. Insurance carriers will typically pay $15.00 to $25.00 per day over the same period of time that they would owe for a rental car. This additional payment will be added to your total loss payment, and this additional money may help you to purchase a replacement vehicle.

Documents Involved in a Total Loss Claim

Once a price is agreed upon, the insurance carrier will require you to convey the title of the vehicle to the insurance company. This is in your best interest. You should not be obligated for ongoing property tax payments if the vehicle is no longer with you.

The documents used to complete the total loss transaction include the bill of sale and odometer statement, the power of attorney, and the certificate of title. If you have financing on the vehicle, the bank holds your certificate of title. In these cases, you would sign an authorization allowing payment directly to the finance company and authorizing the finance company to release title directly to the insurance carrier.

Many clients are concerned when they are asked to sign a power of attorney in a total loss claim. This document is safe to sign. Under North Carolina law, the property damage claim is entirely separate from the personal injury claim. Even if the insurance carrier sneaks hidden release language into the property damage documents, these releases are illegal, null, and void. The purpose of the power of attorney is to allow the insurance carrier to directly apply for transfer of title. Our Department of Motor Vehicles can be very strict when considering title application documents. If there is any error or concern with the paperwork, the DMV will reject the title transfer application. The power of attorney allows the insurance carrier to resubmit applications and complete the title transfer process without your involvement.

Retaining Your Salvage Vehicle

A total loss claim is essentially a forced sale. They pay the full fair market value of the vehicle and take possession of the damaged vehicle. Once the insurer secures legal title, they will then sell the damaged vehicle through auction to recover a portion of their payout. This is the typical and recommended approach. However, as owner, you do have the legal right to retain the damaged vehicle after the total loss claim is closed.

If you choose to retain salvage, the insurance carrier will reduce the amount they pay you for your total loss claim by the amount they estimate as the fair market value of the damaged vehicle in its post-accident condition. Salvage value is typically determined by securing bids from experienced wholesalers and parts dealers.

If you intend to keep the damaged vehicle, the adjuster will determine the value of the wreckage. Once the adjusters determine salvage value, they then reduce your total loss value/payment by the salvage value. If you wish to confirm the adjuster's salvage value determination, you have the legal right to request the name, address, and contact information for the salvage dealers who offered bids to purchase the vehicle for the amount indicated by the adjuster (11 NCAC 04.0418(3)).

If you do retain salvage, the insurance adjuster will notify the Department of Motor Vehicles and a salvage notation will be made on the vehicle title. This would significantly decrease the resale value of the vehicle if you do repair and later sell it. Unless you have significant experience with vehicle repairs or a true need for the undamaged parts on your vehicle, it is typically best to avoid salvage retention.

Unique Vehicle Cases

All of the information in this chapter regarding handling of repair and total loss claims applies even when the damaged vehicle is unique. However, additional issues and concerns should be considered in the following cases.

Rare and Collectible Cars

If you own a vintage automobile or an exotic, you should be extremely careful when choosing a repair facility. Make sure the repair facility is prepared to return the vehicle to its true pre-accident condition. While these specialty shops can be more expensive, the responsible insurance carrier owes to *indemnify* you, which means they must return you to your pre-accident condition. If you own a unique vehicle, truly proper and skillful repairs would be the only way to put you back into the ownership position you held before the accident occurred.

Diminution of value will also be typically much higher in cases involving vintage, collectible, and exotic vehicles. In these cases, you should always secure a certified appraisal by an independent appraiser who has significant experience determining diminution of value for unique vehicles. If the insurance carrier does not honor your estimate, you want to make sure that your appraiser's credentials would solidify your chance of success in a later trial.

Motorcycles

The process of handling a total loss in a motorcycle case is identical to a total loss for a private passenger auto. However, there are unique considerations in the repair process. Motorcycles are not subject to body repair. Rather, the bike repair facility will handle collision repair entirely through new part replacement. Motorcycle repairs do not involve use of body filler, dent repair, or painting. Instead, every damaged part is replaced with a new part. The result is the repair process is *very* expensive and most motorcycle crashes therefore result in total loss. If the bike is repaired, you should be very pleased with the end result because every damaged part will be replaced with new equipment.

Scooters and Mopeds

Like motorcycles, scooters would not be subject to collision repair. Instead, only new parts would be used to replace every damaged component on a moped or scooter. These vehicles are relatively low value in the new and used market. Thus, most crashes do result in a total loss.

Scooters and mopeds do retain their value quite well. If you are dealing with one of these total loss cases, you should perform careful research through local newspapers and online sources such as Craigslist. If your research supports a higher value than the adjuster's offer, they will often include your research in the claim file and increase the amount they pay for your damaged scooter. In most cases, the adjuster handling a scooter total loss will offer full/fair payment from the outset.

Bicycles

The injury aspect of a bicycle accident claim is handled the same as a pedestrian impact. Injuries can be quite severe, and the rider should be extremely careful in all discussions with property damage insurance adjusters. They will pay fairly for the bicycle, but they are looking for inroads to later reduce their payment for the injury claims.

Bicycle sales have continued to trend upward, and we see many unique bicycles on the market today. If your bicycle is specialized, you should work with a local dealer to determine repair cost versus replacement cost. The insurance carriers do owe for the reasonable cost of the latest technology if your bicycle is unique and rare. For example, featherweight carbon fiber frames sell for thousands of dollars in the secondary market, and this full amount should be paid by the insurance company. Also, all repairs should be undertaken entirely with identical or equivalent replacement parts. Make sure your bicycle is restored fully in function, weight, technology, and value.

CHAPTER 5

❖

INJURY CLAIMS

Author's Words of Warning

Many people choose to handle their injury claims without an attorney. This is certainly your right. However, there are advantages to attorney representation. There are also significant risks to handling your case alone, without the advice and guidance of counsel.

Before I explain the injury claim process, I must first make it clear that a single book could never provide complete or proper legal advice for every case. Injury claims are always unique, and your rights depend on your particular injuries and circumstances. Also, as a licensed attorney, I am not allowed to provide legal representation through a broad writing or textbook. For proper legal advice that fits your unique needs and circumstances, you must speak directly with an experienced personal injury lawyer.

While I cannot write a book that acts as everyone's lawyer, I do seek to provide helpful advice to all collision victims facing significant injury. After working for several years as an insurance adjuster and an insurance company lawyer, I realized that insurance companies commonly underpay injury claims. Their main weapon is superior knowledge. I hope, through this work, to empower accident victims and to help innocent victims gain equal bargaining power.

My law firm currently employs four licensed claims adjusters with over eighty years of collective experience handling injury claims for insurance companies. I personally also have years of experience working for insurance companies as a claims adjuster and as an insurance defense lawyer. Our insurance team worked together on this project to help you understand how the other side will look at your case.

In this chapter I reveal many of the secrets and steps involved in the injury claim process. As an attorney committed to enforcing the legal rights of accident victims, I must share the benefits of legal representation in these cases. Attorneys typically pay for themselves in serious injury cases. We also protect your compensation rights, and, through medical expertise and financial leverage, we increase settlement offers and trial verdicts. While the attorney's fee takes a share of the end payment, if we make that payment much larger, we handle all the work, expand your legal options, and work to increase the net payment you receive for your injuries even after the attorney's fee is paid.

How Attorneys Increase Injury Claim Payments

- *Validate the Threat of Trial*—Following an accident, victims have no guaranteed payment rights. Rather, they only have a right to sue the at-fault parties. If you handle your claim without counsel, insurance adjusters know immediately that you intend to settle. They know you don't want a trial, and therefore, they are not motivated to pay what they believe you might win in court.
- *Know and Support True Case Value*—Adjusters know that unrepresented victims typically have no idea what their case is worth. Trial attorneys who commonly handle and research jury trials know what a jury would give you. Thus, we are prepared to properly price the case and push for full value.
- *Control Defense Costs*—Adjusters know your lawyer *will* sue. If suit is filed, their costs skyrocket. If the insurance company refuses to offer a fair settlement and we win that amount at trial, they now must pay the victim and they pay for a lawyer to defend the at-fault driver(s) and they pay 8 percent interest on top of your verdict

and they must hire and pay for their own doctors and medical experts and they may also have to pay for your trial costs. Simply put, lawyers show that settlement on *your* terms is the insurance company's cheapest way out.

- *Control Insurance Communications*—Once you hire a lawyer, it is illegal for a claims adjuster to contact you directly by mail, telephone, or personal visit. Attorneys halt adjuster contacts and their efforts to collect information that will later be used against you. Lawyers deny access to your past medical records and unrelated, private information. Your attorney will also collect, interpret, and highlight your medical evidence to prove the full impact and true extent of all injuries.

- *Locate Hidden Defendants*—Crashes are often caused by multiple factors. If another driver or an outside party contributed to causing your accident, all of these extra parties and their insurance carriers can be legally compelled to contribute toward payment of victim damages.

- *Overcome Liability Defenses*—Adjusters try to blame you for the accident or for failing to follow medical advice. Attorneys properly oppose these arguments and refuse to allow the insurance company to control case valuation.

- *Overcome Medical Causation Arguments*—Adjusters argue that injuries are preexisting and not caused by the accident. They also accuse victims of exaggerating symptoms. Through law and advocacy, attorneys defuse these arguments to avoid erosion of case value.

- *Master All Medical Issues*—The best injury attorneys have considerable medical knowledge and direct access to doctors and medical experts. Injury claims bring full payment only when *all* medical evidence is highlighted for the patient's benefit. With medical support, your lawyer will explain the risks involved in your surgery or medical care, the future problems that might arise, the true nature and extent of all injuries, the effect of injury on overall health and life span, lost quality of life due to injury, and the need and cost of future medical care.

- ***Build and Highlight Admissible Injury Evidence***—Experienced injury lawyers help by building and highlighting all of the evidence that a jury would hear in court. Evidence law is commonly used by insurance companies to exclude information that would motivate more generous verdicts. Attorneys easily avoid these pitfalls. Most cases settle, but your adjuster will only offer *full* value after they are forced to consider all admissible evidence that would motivate a jury to provide the most generous verdict. Personal injury trial lawyers know how to properly present the best evidence to compel higher settlement offers.

- ***Applying Detailed Law of Damages***—Adjusters and insurance companies will not help you find reasons why they should pay you more money. The law of damages is quite complex and constantly changing. Injury lawyers know what can be collected. A detailed demand of everything *legally* due will vastly increase insurance offers and injury payments.

- ***Prove and Collect Future Medical Care Costs***—Insurance companies never pay for future medical problems without proper proof. Attorneys know how to secure focused medical evidence of prognosis to compel full payment for future medical care costs and for future pain and suffering.

- ***Build and Present Proper Income Loss Evidence***—If injuries cause physical disability, future lost wages are awarded in court only if proper evidence confirms lost future earning ability or likely early retirement. Attorneys know how to retain vocational rehabilitation experts and economic experts to prove the full measure of all past and future lost earnings.

- ***Coordinate Health Insurance Filings***—Proper use of personal health insurance can vastly increase your net share of the injury settlement. Attorneys help to prioritize and time filings for personal health insurance, medical payments insurance, and liability insurance. In many cases, you can legally collect *multiple payments* for the same medical charges.

- ***Fight Claims Against Your Settlement***—Health insurance companies and other outside parties often have a hidden right to take money from your settlement. Child support liens, VA liens, workers' compensation, and other payment sources can also take a share of your injury claim and sue you if you fail to pay them. Attorneys help to minimize claims against your injury money. Attorneys should also negotiate unpaid medical bills to reduce what you must pay for medical care not covered by health insurance. Every penny your attorney saves falls directly into your pocket.

Lawyers also have significant advantage handling certain tasks. For example, when requesting medical records and answers to important medical questions, it is best to allow your lawyer to handle all medical inquiries. Doctors are busy, and they typically shy away from lawsuits. If you ask for case-related information during medical appointments, your doctors will document this in your treatment records. Adjusters and insurance defense lawyers look for notations in medical records, such as "patient comes in requesting information for lawsuit" or "possible pecuniary gain motive." Whenever they find these notes, they use them to suggest that your primary reason for the medical appointment was to inflate the value of your accident claim.

Lawyers make medical requests in a way that protects your privacy, avoids negative impact on your medical file, and minimizes inconvenience on your physician's schedule. Your lawyer's medical requests are timely and focused in a way that helps the doctor to provide the best possible evidence and, at the same time, avoid depositions and trials.

Another key benefit of hiring a lawyer is simplicity. You work with doctors toward a full recovery, and your lawyer handles *all* other aspects of your case. The attorney's involvement should increase case value and make the insurance claim process much easier for you. Also, if you intend to hire a lawyer, do so as soon as possible so you can enjoy the maximum protection, benefits, and convenience of legal representation.

Nature of the Injury Claim

In this chapter, you will discover the proper approach to medical care, the path you should follow throughout the injury claim process, and the steps that insurance carriers take to evaluate and pay these claims. Whether you hire an attorney or not, you should respond to all injuries and medical needs and secure thorough and proper medical treatment. The steps you take along the way will protect your health and your legal rights.

If you are injured because of the negligence (careless acts) of another person or entity (e.g., a business or a government official), the law allows you to collect payment from all responsible parties. In most cases, insurance companies represent the responsible parties and handle evaluation and payment of your claims.

Insurance companies are profit-motivated, and they challenge all injury claims. Injury adjusters seek to pay less by arguing that their insured was not at fault, that the injuries claimed were not caused by the accident, that the injuries are less severe than the victim alleges, that some/all medical care was not necessary, that medical care costs were inflated and unreasonable, that the injury will not be lasting or permanent, that income loss was not necessary, and that the value of the injury claim is less than the victim seeks.

Legally speaking, an accident victim truly receives nothing more than a *cause of action*, or a right to sue. Thus, proper determination of the value of an injury claim requires careful consideration of the evidence that a jury would see in court and the likely verdict range of your case at trial.

The individual types of losses and damages that can be collected will be addressed in careful detail throughout this chapter. If you present all claims supported by proper evidence, and if you can motivate all parties and insurance carriers to come forward with an offer of payment that approximates what you would win in court, you can settle the injury claim privately, without court involvement. Settlement of an injury claim is a contractual agreement. The right to a jury trial is forfeited in exchange for a lump-sum payment that all parties agree to.

In this chapter, we review everything that should be paid through settlement, recommended timing of settlement, and the legal affect and finality of settlement. If settlement cannot be reached, trial of your case is the only way to truly compel payment. The litigation and trial process is covered in detail in chapter 7.

Summary of Damages Owed to the Injury Victim

If you are injured because of the negligence of others, you are entitled to collect for damaged personal property, vehicle damage, and for personal injury. On the injury claim, you are entitled to collect for:

- accident-related medical expenses incurred up to the date of settlement or trial
- future medical expenses only if established by sufficient medical evidence
- lost wages up to the date of settlement or trial when work is missed purely for *medical* reasons
- lost earning capacity—future lost earnings for the victim who cannot continue in their previous line of work
- lost work life expectancy—payment for future lost wages when expert testimony confirms that accident-related injuries will require early retirement
- tax-free compensation for pain and suffering endured up to the date of settlement or trial (focus here on full impact of injuries on day-to-day quality of life)
- future pain and suffering only in cases where proper expert medical testimony confirms anticipated future symptoms and complications
- lump-sum payment for scarring and disfigurement
- payment to modify home, vehicle, and workplace to adapt to injury or disability
- payment for assistance with household chores and other services

- any additional loss or expense arising from injury or medical care

Every case must be looked at carefully. Occasionally, other damages can be presented. For example, if a family's medical needs or income loss force them to withdraw money from retirement plans and pay tax penalties, these losses can be claimed and collected.

Maintain the Threat of Trial

The victim's goal is to settle the case. However, insurance carriers know that most people have no intention of going to court. As a former claims adjuster, I assure you that your adjuster must believe that you will bring your case through trial before he or she will offer a proper settlement. This is a primary reason why attorneys see higher settlement offers compared to unrepresented accident victims. If you are handling your case without a lawyer, remain diplomatic and professional in all discussions and make it clear that you will retain counsel and bring your case to trial if necessary. This should be your approach and posture from day one.

How to Approach Initial Medical Treatment

After an accident, your first priority should be to recover your health as soon as possible. Take great care to secure proper diagnosis of *all* injuries and thorough medical care from the very best physicians.

Collision Scene and First Responder Treatment

More serious collisions typically involve EMS, police, and fire-rescue response to the accident scene. The victim has little choice regarding care, but this first phase of medical care is vital. Victims and attorneys often overlook the details involved in collision scene care. You should carefully revisit the ambulance call report, the police report, and the hospital records to highlight compelling injury evidence and to fully understand the initial course of trauma care.

Failure to report injury to police will not bar future injury claims. Honest accident victims who do not have obvious cuts or injury often will report that they are doing well. Adrenaline may overshadow symptoms. Also, many types of injuries (especially soft-tissue injuries) typically first produce the full measure of symptoms during the twenty-four- to forty-eight-hour period following the initial trauma. Thus, it is medically appropriate to experience an onset or progression of symptoms after you have returned home.

The police report and the ambulance call report are the two primary documents evidencing injury at the collision scene. The police report will document your subjective report of injury to the officer at the bottom of page one. This is a coded response, and the notation simply shows the officer's recollection of your experience. The officer will also indicate whether EMS was called to the scene and list all parties who were taken from the scene by ambulance.

The ambulance call report is a combined bill and medical report. This document should be carefully read and interpreted. Emergency medical technicians will document all symptoms, describe the extent of damage to the vehicles involved, note relevant medical history, describe patient appearance, and outline all medical care provided and all injuries managed during ambulance transport. The names of each emergency medical technician (EMT) will also be identified.

Consider follow-up communication with EMTs, especially in serious or catastrophic injury cases. They can be wonderful, helpful witnesses whenever insurance adjusters seek to trivialize the accident or your injury experience. In a trial setting, the EMT who comforted you and stabilized you through transport is a primary witness to the fear, pain, and complications you experienced immediately after the collision.

Some victims refuse ambulance transport and instead travel to the hospital by private vehicle. Ambulance transport is not required to establish a right to fair compensation for personal injury. It is wise to seek medical evaluation as soon as possible following an accident. Further, hospital care is preferred because they have access to lab testing, blood testing, CT and MRI scanning, X-rays, and a battery of specialized physicians, including trauma surgeons and orthopedic surgeons.

In less serious injury cases, ongoing hospitalization will not be required. In fact, many victims feel that their treatment is not sufficiently thorough in hospital emergency departments. The hospital is typically trying to rule out fracture, head and brain injury, or internal organ damage. They are seeking to determine whether ongoing hospitalization is necessary. If not, they will discharge the patient the same day.

Be mindful of all hospital discharge instructions. Hospitals always instruct the patient to secure further evaluation and treatment through family doctors, specialists, or your primary-care physician. Written discharge instructions typically state "patient advised to return to emergency department or seek further care through his or her primary care physician if symptoms persist or worsen." If no follow-up care occurs, insurance adjusters use the discharge instructions as proof that no symptoms continued after the hospital visit.

Hospital records should be scrutinized page by page to isolate all medical notations that support the claim of traumatic injury. Nurses' notes, lab reports, and detailed physician reports should be integrated for later presentation in the injury case. These records should not simply be turned over to the insurance adjuster for review. Adjusters will not help you to unearth the medical details that support higher case value. The victim should carefully interpret hospital records and highlight the record so the adjuster is forced to consider case-supportive details.

If you choose not to go to a hospital, this is absolutely your right and this approach should not devalue the injury case. Many people have established relationships with family doctors, and turning toward a familiar medical provider may be your best option. Be certain that you report every area of injury and every symptom you are dealing with. A family physician can then order X-rays and other diagnostic testing. Whenever necessary, he or she will also refer you to specialists for appropriate evaluation and follow-up treatment.

How to Pay for Thorough Medical Care

One of the first challenges and questions is how to properly pay for accident-related medical care. Ambulance services are often not covered by health insurance, and EMS providers are also aggressive bill collectors. Also, while hospitals will bill for services, follow-up care providers typically want payment first before they agree to see you. The following payment options should be considered as you seek clinical care for all injuries:

At-Fault Driver's Liability Insurance

This is actually the *last* source of payment for medical care. We consider it first to confront the most common mistake made by innocent accident victims. Many people resist using their personal health insurance and instead try to insist that the at-fault driver's car insurance should be paying for all medical care. While this is legally true in the long run, liability coverage *never* pays for medical bills along the way. They will not receive and pay bills from providers, and they will not reimburse you for bills as they are incurred. Rather, they pay for total medical bills only at time of settlement. They also challenge most charges and typically refuse to pay a significant share of the total bills.

Do not present medical bills to the liability adjuster until all medical care is concluded. The options discussed below are truly the only sources for payment of medical charges during the course of ongoing treatment and recovery. Later in the chapter, we discuss how and when to properly present medical bills and other injury evidence to the insurance carriers who provide liability insurance for all parties who caused your accident.

Private Health Insurance

If you have personal health insurance, whether it is employer provided or privately purchased, you should use this coverage to pay for all medical needs. Hospitals often resist using health insurance because they hope to receive a larger payment by waiting to take a share of your injury claim proceeds. They should be pushed to file for health insurance payments. If you have legal representation, your lawyers should help you with this step. Health insurance is no-fault coverage. Thus, they pay medical expenses regardless of how you became ill. Using your health coverage opens doors, provides access to a network of medical experts, such as orthopedic surgeons and neurologists, and protects your personal credit.

When you collect money for your injuries, the health insurance carrier likely will have the right to be paid back from your settlement proceeds. Thus, please do not worry that your health insurance carrier is falling victim because of your accident. The presence of health insurance will be a tremendous asset as you seek to work with all doctors and specialists to recover your health.

The new Affordable Care Act (ACA) policies are another option for health coverage. Because the preexisting condition exclusion has been removed from all health insurance policies, you now have a right to purchase health coverage after an injury and then use this new policy to pay for health care. These policies will have a right to share in your injury claim proceeds. Also, the discounts and medical charge contract adjustments they take on your medical bills will serve to reduce the medical bills you can collect through settlement or present to a jury at trial.

Medicare and Medicaid

Medicare and Medicaid both provide coverage for accident victims. They also both claim rights to a share of any settlement or verdict you receive in the injury case. Whenever possible, you should use this coverage to pay for accident-related medical bills.

Medicare and Medicaid offices are slow and difficult to deal with. Medicare enjoys very broad rights to control and take money from a personal injury settlement. Further, they will not state and fix their reimbursement claim amount until after a settlement is reached. Thus, the victim will not know his or her net share of any settlement at the time that the gross settlement is reached. We hope to see changes in these difficult laws.

Medicare payments for accident-related medical bills are labeled "conditional payments." The payment is conditional because it is made without recourse only if you have no other source of payment for the subject medical charge. If the bill that they pay is later paid through the injury claim, Medicare's position is that they must then be paid back for that charge. At settlement, take time to review their lien claim, force removal of all charges not related to the accident, and negotiate a discount so Medicare takes less from your injury claim payment.

It is sometimes difficult to use Medicare to pay for accident-related medical visits. Medicare's discounts on doctor bills are growing, and many physicians are turning away new Medicare patients. However, if this is your sole source of health insurance coverage, you should make every effort to use Medicare to pay for all treatment arising from your accident.

Medicaid should not be confused with Medicare. Medicaid often comes into the picture after an accident occurs. Medicaid is need-based health insurance coverage and will be provided only if the patient demonstrates true financial need. Currently, Medicaid recipients cannot have more than $2,000.00 in "spendable resources" in their control at any time. If you are involved in an accident requiring extensive initial hospital care or surgery, your hospital's account representative may visit with you and discuss an application for Medicaid qualification. If you have no other payment options, it is wise to follow this path and allow the hospital to help you qualify for Medicaid coverage.

Medicaid is administered by state offices, and the current rules limit Medicaid's total right of payment from your injury claim proceeds. At present, Medicaid cannot take more than 37.5 percent of the total settlement in cases involving attorney representation. This amount can be reduced further through negotiations and also by showing that additional collision-related medical charges remain due at time of settlement.

Military Benefits and Tricare

Tricare is health insurance that covers military, ex-military, and soldiers' family members. The Tricare card allows easy access to network doctors with only a small copay due at the time of the appointment. Tricare policies apply the same way private health insurance does in injury cases. The differences are at the back end, where the military branch or Tricare seeks reimbursement. If a soldier is injured in an accident and presents a personal injury claim, the branch of the military that provides free medical treatment to the soldier will seek payment for medical care from the outside party who caused the injury. If the injured soldier hires a lawyer, the military compels the attorney to protect the federal government's interest. Thus, in a soldier's injury claim, we often see branches such as the Department of the Navy seeking a signed agreement where the soldier's attorney agrees to also represent the federal government to ensure that the responsible parties pay for medical care provided for injured military personnel.

From the patient's perspective, using Tricare coverage allows visits to nonmilitary medical facilities. These facilities typically maintain more thorough medical records and the doctors in these private-sector clinics are less likely to be transferred far away. Whenever possible, it is best for injured soldiers to seek care outside of the military hospital and military medical network.

Medical Payments Coverage

Medical payments coverage (a.k.a. medpay) is another source of health insurance for motor vehicle accident victims. This is wonderful coverage and should be carefully utilized by every accident victim. Medpay is a portable health insurance policy that is attached to the car insurance policy. Victims often have rights to collect under multiple medpay policies. The primary medpay insurer is the policy that covers the car that the victim occupied at the time of collision. Once that policy is exhausted, the victim can look to other policies in his or her household for additional coverage (see chapter 1 for a detailed description of how to locate and use medpay policies).

Medpay pays the full amount of billed medical expenses. Unlike other health insurance sources, the medpay insurance carrier does *not* have a right to collect reimbursement from your injury settlement. Thus, if you are eligible for medpay coverage, you can collect twice for covered medical expenses thereby netting a higher share of your total injury settlement. If you have health insurance and medpay, the health insurance carrier may have a right to take a share of your medpay as reimbursement for their payment of accident-related medical expenses. Through proper timing and coordination of health insurance and medpay filings, you can reduce the health insurance carrier's reimbursement claims and thereby increase your total share of all insurance benefits and payments.

Workers' Compensation

If you are an innocent accident victim but you also happened to be working when another party causes an auto accident, workers' compensation will be your primary source of health insurance. Workers' comp has certain restrictions that you must follow. For example, you must use the physicians approved by the workers' comp insurance carrier, you must allow workers' comp case workers to attend certain medical appointments, and you must also follow all restrictions imposed by the North Carolina Workers' Compensation Act during the course of care.

Workers' comp is very helpful for accident victims. You may not need an attorney in the workers' comp case, and hiring an attorney to present your personal injury claims against those who caused your accident would not require you to also retain counsel to fight your employer or their workers' comp carrier. However, if the workers' comp carrier is refusing necessary medical care, pushing you back to work too soon, or otherwise restricting benefits, you may prefer to hire counsel in the workers comp' claim as well.

Workers' comp pays for all medical care, and they also pay lump-sum payments for permanent injury and for temporary or permanent income loss due to injury. The workers' comp carrier does have a right to take a share of the injury claim proceeds. In fact, after twelve months have passed, the workers' comp carrier has a right to take control over your personal injury case and hire their own attorney to take the lead. Since the workers' comp carrier's interests are opposed to yours, you should ensure that you or your attorneys maintain control of all claims against drivers and all other parties who caused your injuries.

Seeking Medical Treatment on Private-Pay / Credit Basis

If you do not have health insurance, you must either find physicians who will treat you on a credit basis or seek to purchase health insurance through the current federal programs, which allow health insurance coverage with no exception for preexisting conditions. If you cannot fund a health insurance purchase, you may be eligible for subsidized care or be qualified for Medicaid coverage that essentially provides free medical care for accident victims. Beyond these choices, up-front payment or treatment with doctors who agree to bill you later are your only options.

It can be very difficult to find doctors who will wait for payment. Orthopedic doctors who handle bone and joint injuries commonly insist on prepayment before an initial evaluation. If you are able to set up a payment arrangement, this is acceptable. Ideally, the physician will leave all charges due and owing and accept assurance from your lawyer or the liability insurance carrier that the charges will be paid from injury case proceeds at time of settlement. Attorneys can offer a *letter of protection* to these unpaid physicians, essentially promising to include all charges in the injury case and to pay unpaid charges directly from your settlement/verdict funds. Many doctors respond favorably to a letter of protection. They see your lawyer's involvement as confirmation of the validity of the injury claim, and they also see that your lawyer is promising to protect the doctor's right to payment directly from your insurance claim proceeds.

Chiropractors commonly provide medical treatment to accident victims on a credit basis. They understand that North Carolina follows a single, lump-sum approach to payment of injury claims. They know that their bills are considered and paid after all treatment is concluded, and they will typically work with patients and provide care without up-front charges or ongoing payment obligations.

Free clinics and other subsidized care facilities can also be very helpful for those with no health coverage. The downside is these clinics often only provide general family medicine, and they are not well suited to deal with serious or lasting injuries.

Despite the money challenges, you should explore every option and make sure that you receive careful medical attention, full diagnosis of all injuries, and thorough medical treatment until you have reached a full recovery. This approach protects your health and supports important legal rights.

Proper Medical Care & Your Injury Claim

Regardless of how you are able to fund medical care, please understand that it is vitally important to your health and to your legal case that you secure complete medical care. Accident victims who do not seek medical care will not be paid for their injuries and suffering. When adjusters consider how much to pay for pain and suffering, they *always* look at the dollar value of your medical bills, at the nature of your medical treatment, and at all of the medical records that document your symptoms and your course of treatment. Your medical treatment will be the focus of the personal injury case. Thus, the steps you take to recover your health under doctors' care will also generate proper medical records and evidence of the full extent of all injuries. This evidence will motivate a fairer and more generous settlement in your injury case.

Report All Symptoms to Your Doctors

It is imperative that you report every slight symptom and problem to your doctors as early as possible following a collision. Insurance adjusters who evaluate and pay injury claims always question and challenge these cases. If there is a significant delay in reporting an injury, insurance adjusters typically deny these claims by arguing that the injury or condition was not caused by the accident.

If you have a significant primary injury and fail to report less serious injuries until a later date, adjusters commonly question whether these secondary injuries were caused by your accident. If they deny voluntary payment, this forces you to file a lawsuit and conduct a jury trial to collect fair payment for your injuries. If you report *all* symptoms, including secondary difficulties, such as sleep loss or emotional difficulties, this will allow your doctors to understand the full impact of the collision-related injuries on your overall health and quality of life. Reporting all symptoms will also help doctors to properly diagnose and treat your injuries.

While your legal claims are less important than your personal health, your diligent effort to report all symptoms and secure thorough medical treatment will generate proper and thorough medical evidence. This documentation will allow you or your attorneys to secure a generous settlement or verdict, which provides proper compensation for all of the injuries and difficulties the collision caused in your life.

Follow the Medical Path to Conclusion

An accident victim who leaves the collision scene by ambulance has very little choice concerning medical options. Following any forceful collision, hospital evaluation is wise. However, please understand that hospital protocol is to determine whether any fractures or internal injuries have been suffered that would require ongoing hospitalization. Thus, most accident-related hospital visits are brief and result in discharge of the patient on the incident date. Careful review of your hospital discharge instructions will reveal the emergency room physicians' referral to a specialist or their instruction that you report any ongoing symptoms or difficulties to your personal primary-care physician as soon as possible. Please do not be concerned if your hospital experience seemed brief or incomplete. Instead, follow the suggested path and make sure your personal care physicians deal with all injuries.

Traumatic injury arising from motor vehicle collisions can be terribly severe and disabling. However, in some cases, the early effects of injury are not severe. Some conditions are latent or progressive, causing symptoms that remain latent and then worsen over time. In every case where symptoms continue after several days, you should report as soon as possible to your family doctor who is most familiar with your overall health. Most family physicians deal with general health needs. Thus, if you have suffered any joint injury, nerve injury, internal injury, or fractures or bone injuries, your primary-care physician should refer you to a specialist who is best equipped to confront more serious injuries and restore your health.

Specialists will often refer you for additional related treatment within their own network of treatment providers. For example, orthopedic surgeons confronting herniated disks or spinal injury will often refer the patient for clinical physical therapy. You should follow this path *carefully and attend all recommended clinical visits*. This will allow you the best chance of a complete recovery. Also, you will avoid insurance adjuster accusations that your injuries were not severe, that you were non-compliant with medical advice, and that you caused your own suffering.

Please understand that doctors typically rely on you to determine whether their ongoing medical assistance is needed. If they do not hear from you, they will assume that their past care was sufficient to eliminate all symptoms. If you do not need further medical treatment, you certainly should not waste time and resources seeking unnecessary medical care. However, the more common errors for accident victims are failing to report all symptoms and to follow doctors' advice. Since the medical care will be the financial responsibility of the drivers and insurance carriers who owe for your injury claims, your medical care will ultimately be free of charge.

Please protect your health and follow all directions and suggestions offered by your medical team.

The "Missed Appointment" Trap

Under North Carolina law, the injury victim has a legal duty to mitigate damages. To collect full payment for medical expenses and all other injury claims, you must show that you acted with reasonable care to heal as quickly as possible and to avoid unnecessary expenses or suffering. It is vitally important that you follow all of your doctor's instructions and recommended limitations. Further, it is essential that you attend all recommended medical appointments.

Insurance adjusters are typically friendly immediately after an accident, and they are usually helpful on property damage claims. They will also ask for a medical authorization allowing them access to your personal medical records with every physician. They are not using this authorization to help you build evidence or find reasons to pay more money. To the contrary, they will not help you gather medical records or bills relating to the accident. Instead, they will use the authorization to review your past medical history and private medical information from outside physicians who are not involved in accident-related medical care. You should not allow access to your personal and private medical information.

When insurance adjusters review your claim to place a price on your case, they cherry-pick all of the records and look only for reasons to question all medical claims. A primary focus is missed medical appointments. If your physicians recommend clinical therapy and you reject this or if you miss a number of scheduled appointments, the adjuster will use this evidence to contend that you failed to follow medical advice and that you caused your own suffering. Even though busy schedules may prevent attending all medical appointments, insurance adjusters ignore these practicalities. They will argue that if you truly needed medical care, you would certainly attend all scheduled appointments.

To ensure a thorough recovery and to protect your health and legal rights, you should carefully follow all doctors' advice and attend all scheduled appointments. Whenever possible, take prescribed medication as advised. Also, you should carefully follow physicians' limiting instructions, including lifting restrictions and work-duty restrictions. Careful adherence to medical advice will give you the best chance of a full recovery. Also, your compliance will be evident in your medical records and will support a more generous settlement offer or trial verdict.

The Importance of Medical Specialists

If your injuries cause symptoms or limitations that continue more than four to six weeks, you should speak with your family doctor or primary-care physician about the potential need for specialized care. For example, in a spinal injury case where the patient is experiencing ongoing pain with any numbness or tingling sensation extending from the point of injury into the arms and hands or legs and feet, it is typically wise for a family physician to refer the patient for an orthopedic or neurological evaluation. The more specialized physicians deal with these specific injuries on a daily basis. They are highly trained to focus on proper diagnosis and treatment of significant injury.

Many health insurance programs utilize a *preferred provider network*, which is a list of family care physicians and specialists who are all covered under the health insurance policy. With these plans, the primary care physician is the first stop for all general medical needs. A small copay covers full payment for the family doctor visit. Many plans require the patient to first see the primary-care physicians (a.k.a. PCP) and then secure their referral to a specialist. This is an insurance-related cost-control safeguard. Please understand, therefore, that you should make sure that you are moving past the family physician who deals with general medical needs and securing the opinions, diagnosis, and care of specialists if injuries are severe or lasting.

Traumatic injury arising from motor vehicle collision often involves care with the following types of medical specialists:

- **Orthopedic Surgeons**—Orthopedic and sports medicine specialists deal with fractures, bone injuries, ligament damage, and joint injuries.
- **Neurologists and Neurosurgeons**—Neurological physicians deal with nerve injuries and brain injuries. Orthopedists and neurologists can both handle spinal injuries as the two practice areas overlap for this area of the body.
- **Podiatrists**—Foot and ankle injuries are quite typical especially in head-on crashes. Podiatrists only treat foot conditions, and they understand how foot injuries can affect overall health. In cases involving fracture, orthopedists often working alongside podiatrists to treat the foot injury.
- **Reconstructive and Plastic Surgeons**—In cases of scarring or burns, plastic surgeons are best suited to determine how to minimize the appearance of scars. They typically cannot confirm the best treatment options until scars have healed for twelve months. If the patient has pain or numbness around the scar, a neurologist may also be involved to assess and treat nerve damage caused by the underlying wound.
- **Dentists and Maxillofacial Surgeons**—Face and head trauma often produces injuries to the jaw and teeth. Dental or orthodontic care is often sufficient to repair this damage. In more severe cases, a maxillofacial surgeon may be involved. Following repairs, a future care plan should be prepared to allow collection of future dental charges. Most dental repairs are not sufficient to last a lifetime, and the victim should have money now to cover future needs.
- **Physical Therapists**—In most bone and joint injury cases, physical therapy is recommended by the orthopedic surgeon to restore range of motion and strength and to eliminate pain. This care is particularly beneficial and should be carefully followed by the patient.
- **Chiropractors**—There is some debate regarding the efficacy and propriety of chiropractic care. Chiropractic treatment certainly has provided significant benefit for many patients. Insurance adjusters and insurance defense lawyers challenge chiropractic credentials and suggest that they are not full medical doctors. It may be wise,

106

therefore, to allow your primary-care physician or orthopedist to oversee chiropractic care and confirm that this treatment is recommended. Chiropractors typically provide medical care on a credit basis. In the absence of health insurance, this is an excellent option to confront spinal and whiplash injuries.

- *Ophthalmologists*—Eye injuries can be tragic. Ophthalmologists and eye surgeons can help to restore damage to the lenses, cornea, retina, optic nerve, and other components of the patient's eye.

- *Internists and General Surgeon*—Injuries to the internal organs can be life threatening. Internists are often involved from the initial course of patient hospitalization. These specialists can deal with abdominal injuries, organ damage, and other systemic internal injuries.

- *Psychiatrists and Psychologists*—Emotional trauma arising from serious collisions can change the course of a patient's life. Chronic pain can lead to sleep loss and clinical depression. Also, catastrophic collisions commonly result in post-traumatic stress disorder. While post-accident anxiety is somewhat common and while mild anxiety often resolves with time and perspective, psychological therapy and psychiatric care is sometimes the only way for a patient to recover emotional stability following an accident.

- *Cognitive Therapists and Neuropsychologists*—Blunt-force trauma to the head can result in diffuse organic brain damage. These physicians evaluate, quantify, and treat closed head injury. Following head trauma or concussion, patients sometimes experience an inability to remember important facts, inability to organize thoughts, loss of long-term and/or short-term memory, mood swings, and frightening personality changes. These specialists help to properly diagnose and overcome these injuries.

- *Cardiologists*—Trauma to the heart can be life threatening. Further, blunt chest trauma can increase health risks for patients already under cardiac care. These specialists document and treat collision-related heart damage.

- *Vascular Surgeons*—Deep wounds and severe blunt-force trauma can result in damage to veins, arteries, and the circulatory system.

Vascular surgeons are typically called in to join the trauma care team when collision produces injuries requiring emergency surgery.

- ***Pain Management Specialists***—These physicians provide permanent, ongoing care for patients who have chronic pain. Some injuries and medical conditions result in unavoidable pain on a daily basis. Pain management doctors determine a patient-specific plan for therapy and medicine that provides the safest and most effective reduction of chronic pain. Pain management plans should be carefully prepared to ensure that the victim collects all money needed for a lifetime of medically ordered pain relief.

- ***Pulmonologists***—These specialists deal with injury to the lungs and respiratory system. Collapsed lung and other related injuries are common in vehicle collisions. A pulmonologist will treat these injuries and also help to document any permanent effects.

- ***Physiatrists***—These physicians look at the global and systemic effect of injury on the patient's overall health. Where an orthopedic surgeon steps in to repair a fracture, the physiatrist follows the patient after recovery, considers the effect of medicine on organ function, and is best suited to evaluate the need for future medical care and the future complications and symptoms that arise from the injury and any medications utilized during the healing process.

Recovering your health should be your first priority. By working with the proper team of medical providers, you will have the best chance of a rapid and complete recovery. Also, medical care records from specialists serve as the best and most thorough evidence in the personal injury case. This unimpeachable evidence of the nature and extent of injury gives you or your lawyers clear and compelling evidence to motivate the highest possible settlement offers or trial verdicts.

The Injury Claim Process

Dangers of Early Settlement and Scheduled Releases

Always avoid early and premature injury claim settlements. Insurance companies love to settle potentially severe injury claims very early in the process. They will offer "scheduled releases" and other early payment opportunities that are typically a terrible mistake for the injury victim. Frankly, the scheduled release should be an illegal and unenforceable contract. However, many carriers use these.

A scheduled release is an offer to pay a small lump-sum payment immediately (typically in the range of $250.00 to $1,500.00) plus an agreement to independently pay for future medical care. The lump-sum cash amount typically depends on the severity of the accident and the potential severity of the injury. Insurance adjusters often imply that they are offering this money as a courtesy and they will ask the victim to sign the scheduled release, which contains the insurance carrier's promise to pay up to a certain amount for medical expenses over a specified period of time. Never consider these agreements unless you are certain that you have *no* lasting injuries!

There are hidden dangers in these insurance contracts. Remember that a release is a contract and marks the end of your case. Settlements are *final*! Thus, do not forfeit your rights until you know you have been fairly compensated.

Hidden Traps in the Scheduled Release

The four hidden rip-offs in the scheduled release are as follows:

1. ***Improper time limit for medical expense coverage***—Scheduled releases typically limit the insurer's obligation to pay for medical expenses to a period of six to twelve months following the accident. They actually owe for accident-related medical care for the rest of your life. They get these early agreements so that they can

later deny payment of valid medical expenses incurred after the deadline imposed by the scheduled release.

2. ***Unfair dollar limit on medical expense obligation***—Adjusters seeking scheduled releases are trained to offer an apparently reasonable dollar amount for future medical expenses, which would *not* include specialized care or any payment for unforeseen medical problems or chronic symptoms. The at-fault driver and his or her insurance carriers owe the full cost of all accident-related medical care over the patient's lifetime. While you may agree to accept a lower sum later, you should never put a cap and barrier on the insurance company's financial obligations for the full cost of all medical treatment ultimately required.

3. ***Small print "reasonable charge" restriction***—If you sign a scheduled release and present medical bills that fall within the dollar value restriction, insurance carriers commonly red-line the bills and refuse to pay the full amount of your medical charges. They rely on small print in the scheduled release contract, which states that the insurance carrier only owes "reasonable" medical charges. When you present your bills for payment, they will compare billed amounts to their internally prepared list of approved and reasonable charges. If they disagree with your doctor's charges, they refuse to pay the full amount of your medical bills. Essentially, this takes back the small amount of money you received when you signed the scheduled release agreement.

4. ***Small print "necessary charge" restriction***—Insurance carriers also refuse full payment of medical expenses by questioning the true need for medical care. For example, if you have physical therapy three times per week, they may argue that only two visits were "necessary." They then simply refuse payment for care that they conclude was not necessary. Again, you receive significantly less than the full amount of your bills. Accident victims who sign these agreements often end up owing more for medical expenses than they received through the early, insufficient up-front payment.

Settlement—Timing and Deadlines

The statutory deadline for filing a lawsuit in a personal injury case is three years after the collision occurs. If the accident results in fatal injury, the claim becomes a case for wrongful death benefits. This specific type of claim is governed by statute, and the lawsuit filing deadline is two years from the date of accident.

The timing of initial presentation and negotiation of injury claims varies considerably with every case. As a general rule, it is best to settle your case after you have been released from all medical care. This approach allows you to ensure that all injuries and medical treatment are considered at the time of settlement. This is the safest and most common approach.

In cases involving severe injury, it is occasionally wise to consider settlement options much earlier in the case. For example, most health insurance plans have a legal right of reimbursement and they can collect reimbursement directly from your settlement proceeds. If the at-fault driver does not have high coverage, or if we are limited to just one or two automobile liability insurance policies, we may see that the available insurance coverage is less than the likely verdict range of the case.

Further, since the amount of the health insurance reimbursement claim depends on the amount of health care benefits paid up to the time of settlement, it is often wise to present a forceful demand for disclosure and payment of all liability insurance early in the case. If the responsible driver does not have significant personal wealth, real estate, or other assets, and if the liability insurance is limited, early settlement allows early payment of the health insurance lien claim. If you are able to pay the health insurance carrier *before* they have paid the lion's share of bills, you may pay a much lower reimbursement lien amount to the health insurance carrier. Simply put, in cases involving severe injury, we often net the accident victim much more money by settling before all medical care is concluded.

In cases involving chronic injury requiring medical care extending beyond the three-year suit-filing deadline, it is wise to explore settlement options before the patient concludes medical care. Some victims will always be under medical care. Thus, it is impossible to wait until medical treatment is concluded before settling the case or bringing the matter to trial. In these cases, medical experts and vocational rehabilitation experts are hired to prepare a life care plan. This is a very detailed report that documents the treating physicians' prediction and itemization of all future care expected for the patient over the balance of the victim's lifetime. Vocational rehabilitation specialists and economists then work to show the true cost of all future medical needs and all other costs associated with adapting the patient's home and lifestyle to his or her injuries. The economic expert then reduces the list of anticipated future costs to a present monetary value. This chain of evidence is required to support any claim for payment of future medical needs.

Severe and catastrophic injury cases should only be handled by experienced attorneys. It is essential that the evidence presented would be qualified and accepted as admissible at trial. Further, careful selection of trial experts and careful presentation of this evidence will help to overcome anticipated insurance challenges and ensure that these large monetary claims are properly honored and paid.

Proper Injury Case Presentation

Insurance adjusters will not help you to highlight your medical evidence, build your injury case, or isolate reasons why they should pay you more money. Instead, they try to focus only on the weaknesses of the injury claim. When they consider how much to pay, they look at the strength of your legal team, your apparent willingness to bring the case through trial, and all of the evidence that a jury would see in a trial setting.

Every victim prefers a private settlement. However, you should not settle unless all responsible parties come forward with a payment offer that reflects what you would win at trial. Getting them to this point is the challenge.

Elements of Evidence in the Injury Claim

If suit has not been filed, the injury claim documentation will be presented directly to all insurance companies who represent the at-fault driver(s). In hit-and-run accidents and cases involving uninsured drivers, the victim presents the claim directly to their own insurance carrier. Please understand that, in these cases, your insurance carrier will behave as though the uninsured or hit-and-run driver was actually insured by your carrier. Even though you collect under your own policy, the adjuster will oppose and question your claims and will treat you just as though you had no insurance with that company. In fact, if your case cannot be settled and goes to trial, the uninsured motorist coverage under your policy will pay for the lawyer who defends the uninsured driver and who opposes your claims in court.

If you handle your claims without counsel, the insurance adjuster will control the process of injury claim presentation. Adjusters typically demand that the claimant/victim sign a medical authorization. Attorneys typically refuse these authorizations because you are not legally obligated to provide access to your private, unrelated medical information. Nevertheless, if you handle your injury claim without counsel, adjusters typically insist on these authorizations and refuse to consider injury claims or negotiate settlement without direct access to your medical history.

The unrepresented claimant should present his or her claim in the same fashion that an experienced personal injury attorney would. You are working toward a settlement that is a single lump-sum payment, including all past and future medical expenses, all past and future lost wages, all other expenses and financial losses relating to the injury, and payment for past and future pain and suffering. To collect for all damages, the settlement demand brochure must be a carefully organized presentation of all evidence that would be presented at trial to support the highest verdict and award.

The victim has the burden to collect and offer proof of all damages. Insurance adjusters will not help you find valuable evidence, and they will not look for reasons to pay you more money. Thus, you must do the legwork to carefully unearth and properly present all medical evidence and anecdotal evidence to show the severity of your injury, the full cost of medical care, the amount of all lost income and earning ability, and the true impact of injuries on your quality of life.

While some cases call for unique evidentiary presentations, the following elements of proof are typically included in a thorough and properly prepared personal injury demand brochure:

- *police report and summary of collision evidence*—While many parts of the police report are inadmissible in a personal injury trial, every settlement demand presentation should include the investigating officer's police report and other official reports, such as state patrol motor carrier enforcement reports in truck and commercial vehicle collision cases. In the case presentation, it is wise to highlight and resolve any substantive errors in police records.

- *collision photos*—Whenever possible, secure photos of all vehicles involved in a motor vehicle accident. Also, photos of the accident scene are helpful in serious injury cases. If you do not personally have these photos, law enforcement may be willing to share their internal notes and photographs. If they are not willing to voluntarily produce these, a subpoena will mandate disclosure.

- *personal and medical background information for victim*—To secure the best payment results, it is important to help the insurance adjusters understand the victim's lifestyle and health status before the accident. If there were prior medical problems, it is often wise to voluntarily disclose this information. The victim should present preexisting conditions as preexisting "frailties." Since the responsible parties owe for any worsening of a prior medical condition, you should open-handedly share this medical background. Also, share positive points about the family picture, whether the victim is a parent of young children, details about your educational and occupational history, a list of hobbies and activities you enjoy, and a summary of your lifestyle before the subject collision.

- *past medical records*—These records are not provided in every case. However, if you had obvious preexisting conditions that were worsened by the accident, insurance adjusters will ask for past medical records. Providing these with the initial demand enhances credibility, streamlines the claim process, and avoids any accusations that your evidence was intentionally incomplete. In back and spinal injury cases, always provide past medical history in cases where the client/victim had no prior problems with back pain or related difficulties. Back pain is a common medical condition. If you had perfect spinal health with no prior symptoms, such as neck pain, back pain, headaches, or similar difficulties, providing the clean medical history compels the adjuster to understand that all post-accident pain was truly caused by the subject collision.

- *accident-related medical bills*—The insurance carrier will insist that you produce all accident-related medical invoices. They will only consider line-item invoicing with ICD-9 diagnostic codes for each treatment modality. Thus, they will not accept the medical bills that are mailed directly to the patient's home. If you are represented, your attorney will handle these details for you. If you are unrepresented, the adjuster will insist that you secure thorough and proper medical invoicing. Your physicians should be glad to provide itemized invoices with diagnostic coding upon request.

- *list of all insurance payments made on medical charges*— Recent legislative changes have vastly decreased the amount accident victims can collect for medical bills. For accidents on and after October 1, 2011, trial evidence of past medical expenses is limited to the actual amounts paid by health insurance carriers. Unfortunately, this hides the true amount of medical bills from your jury, which, in turn, results in a significant reduction in the amount insurance companies will pay for medical expenses. These recent changes now require victims to provide a list of all payments and credits on all medical accounts.

- *medical records with research and injury description*—You or your attorney should collect and review every page from your medical files with all medical providers. It is essential to produce every medical record relating to your treatment. Also, care should be taken to read and interpret these vitally important records. Adjusters will not comb the records for evidence indicating permanency of injury or higher case value. Rather, they cherry-pick the records only looking for notations that suggest that you are doing well or that the injuries are less severe. Medical records should be presented in a carefully organized fashion. A medical summary highlighting all medical notes, nurses' notes, radiology and imaging reports, and other elements that confirm the true nature and extent of all injuries should be included. The medical records are the heart of the injury case. Careful analysis, proper interpretation, and thorough presentation will result in much higher settlement offers and trial verdicts.

- ***injury summary with supportive medical research***—The medical records presentation should be joined with a medical summary that lists and describes all injuries, which includes photographs and supportive references to the patient's medical records and describes problems and treatment associated with each and every injury endured in the accident. Where multiple injuries exist, medical research regarding the overlay of all conditions will best show the cumulative effect of the injuries on the victim's health and mobility.

- ***physicians' disability orders***—If a doctor provides notes ordering the patient to avoid work or to limit work duties, these notes should be included with the settlement demand. These will confirm that missed work occurred for medical reasons and, therefore, all lost wages are legally owed.

- ***physicians' narratives***—Patients should be very cautious when discussing their injury claims and legal matters with their physicians. Your doctors are there to restore your health. They are typically not interested in becoming involved in injury and insurance claims or in litigation or trials. Your sole focus with physicians should be recovering your health. However, in some cases, medical evidence is required to confirm that injuries are indeed related to the accident. Insurance companies challenge the causal relationship between injuries and the accident in almost every case. Medical narratives are commonly needed to show that specific injuries were indeed caused by a collision. Also, whenever an injury produces chronic or permanent symptoms, a qualified medical expert's testimony is the only way to legally prove that the injury is lasting or permanent. Without this evidence, the insurance carrier will not pay for any future medical expenses or for the victim's future pain and suffering. Attorneys are best suited to secure effective medical narratives. Lawyers know exactly which questions to ask and they also help the doctor understand that a clear medical opinion letter will promote settlement. If the physician understands that his or her narrative opinion may motivate a private settlement obviating any need for lawsuits or trial, he or she will typically take the time to provide honest evidence to support the full value of your case.

- ***injury photographs and video***—Photographs of all visible injuries motivate higher settlement offers and trial verdicts. In cases involving lacerations, sutures, surgery, fractures, or other obvious visible injury, photographs should be taken throughout the healing process. This irrefutable evidence overcomes later adjuster arguments that injuries are less significant than claimed. In cases of catastrophic injury, attorneys commonly use "day-in-the-life" videos to show how injury-related incapacitation has impacted the victim's quality of life.

- ***life care plan in catastrophic injury cases***—If medical care will continue well after the three-year lawsuit filing deadline, the settlement demand or trial evidence presentation must include a life-care plan. This plan is prepared by a team of experts, including a vocational rehabilitation specialist, an economist who can reduce future care cost to present monetary value, and the victim's team of attending physicians. The life-care plan is the proper way to quantify and claim compensation for all anticipated future medical needs.

- ***employer certification of lost income***—The victim is entitled to payment for all lost income and wages for work missed because of injury and medical restriction. While the doctor must confirm that you are medically unable to work, evidence must also show that you indeed missed work following the accident. The employer should only document pay rate and time actually missed from work. If you were paid for sick time or vacation and therefore missed no pay, you are still entitled to full payment of lost wages. Thus, the employer's certification should not indicate whether the victim received sick pay or other wage benefits. In cases of self-employed individuals, you must carefully document all lost jobs and income opportunities. Insurance carriers will also typically insist on three years of past income tax filings to confirm the history of earnings in the self-employed enterprise.

- *economic evidence supporting future lost earnings*—If your injuries compelled you to change or accept less pay, medical evidence must confirm that injury-related disability prevented you from continuing in your past work capacity. Employment evidence must also show that the employer discontinued your previous role and document the new/current earnings and the anticipated future earning schedule. In a trial setting, lawyers introduce the expert testimony of a vocational rehabilitation specialist. This expert will confirm that the injuries prevented continued employment in the pre-accident capacity.

- *economist and vocational-rehabilitation expert report*—Detailed expert testimony is required in cases involving permanent income loss, and in any claim for lost work life expectancy. In some cases, the victim may be able to return to work full-time now but later be compelled to retire early because of medical restrictions. Vocational rehabilitation specialists are able to prove and quantify these claims. They look to industrial tables that define the level of physical exertion required in your work, compare that to the medical evidence of permanent restriction, and calculate the anticipated early retirement age for the patient.

- *statement of theory of legal liability*—Insurance carriers are more attentive and generous in response to thoroughly prepared legal demands. When you ask for compensation for personal injury, you should include a presentation of all laws that support your claims for compensation. Here, you list all driving errors, all traffic law violations, and all evidence laws that support your injury claims. If the responsible driver was intoxicated or guilty of intentional conduct, you should also present all laws supporting a claim for punitive damages.

- *summary description of impact of injuries on victim quality of life*—When you present your case, adjusters hope you will just drop off the medical records and allow them to evaluate the claim. They will offer pennies on the dollar in these cases. When you ask for tax-free payment for physical pain and emotional suffering, you must be prepared to share the story of how the accident impacted your life. Offer statements and testimony about missed family vacations, missed opportunities, and the effect of symptoms on your sleep, day-to-day life, and relationships. You should not exaggerate your suffering. However, you should not minimize it either. If the accident happened near the holidays, address how your holidays were impacted.

- *victim's injury journal*—Victims benefit from maintaining a diary to record their experiences and difficulties during the course of treatment and recovery. The journal can be shared in whole or in part and will help to ensure that all difficulties and problems are remembered and shared. If you have a lawyer, begin the journal with the first entry "Dear Attorney." This converts the journal to a privileged attorney-client communication, which allows your lawyers to use only those parts of the journal that they feel will best support your injury claims.

- *monetary demand*—Your injury claim is worth the amount that a jury would award you at trial. Injury cases are valued for settlement purposes by researching trial verdicts in similar cases. Insurance companies seek to negotiate in every case. Thus, it is wise to begin with a settlement demand that is at the high range of negotiations. This leaves room to negotiate and still reach your settlement objectives. If you have no idea of the value of your case, you should avoid placing any dollar value on your claim. Instead, allow the adjuster to evaluate the case and then seek legal advice after you receive a settlement offer. There are extensive dangers negotiating an injury case without counsel. However, some people prefer to handle their claims without a lawyer. If this is your preference, please be very careful stating and fixing the price on your injury case. If you are too low, you may put a ceiling on what your attorney is able to later accomplish. If you are too high, the adjuster will question the credibility of your entire case.

The elements of evidence listed above are common parts of a proper injury case presentation. However, unique circumstances may require additional considerations. For example, in cases involving drunk driving, the at-fault driver's criminal record and driving history should be included as part of the initial demand brochure. The primary goal when preparing the settlement demand brochure is to tell the victim's complete subjective story and medical story through convincing and emotionally compelling evidence.

Who Receives Your Settlement Demand

To determine who receives your settlement demand, you must identify every party who contributed to causing your injuries. You then identify the insurance carrier for each responsible party. The victim's demand with all supportive evidence should then be directed to the adjusters for each individual insurance carrier.

In most car accident cases, the only insurance carrier involved is the liability coverage on the at-fault vehicle(s). However, severe injury cases and more valuable injury claims often pull funding from multiple insurance policies. As a practical matter, the question of who owes for your injuries boils down to a list of all overlapping insurance policies that share the obligation to pay for victim claims. The following is a list of typical insurance sources that contribute to fund injury claim payments:

- *primary auto liability insurance*—The first in line to pay victim claims is the liability insurance on the at-fault driver's vehicle.
- *joint tortfeasors*—If more than one driver contributes to causing your accident, the liability insurance policy covering each at-fault vehicle will share concurrent primary liability for injury claim

payments. For example, if two drivers fail to observe a red light and strike a third driver, the innocent victim collects from the two liability insurance policies covering the two at-fault vehicles.

- *excess liability insurance and umbrella coverage*—For any at-fault driver and vehicle, the auto policy may be augmented by the driver's homeowner's umbrella coverage or by additional liability insurance. Many homeowners will add $1,000,000.00 in excess liability insurance to protect their home and assets in the event of a catastrophic accident. In serious injury cases, make sure that all excess liability insurance policies are involved in settlement discussions.

- *driver personal coverage in borrowed vehicle case*—If a driver borrows a friend's vehicle, the liability insurance policy on the borrowed vehicle provides primary liability insurance. However, if the victim's injury case value exceeds the liability coverage limits on the vehicle policy, the victim can access additional liability insurance coverage through the driver's personal auto insurance policy.

- *at-fault driver's family car insurance policies*—Car insurance covers the "named insured" and any resident relative when they cause a collision. Thus, a driver who causes an accident may be covered by another family member's liability insurance. This excess liability coverage provides additional money to pay the injured party. Victims should review all car insurance policies in the at-fault driver's household to locate additional coverage.

- *business coverage and commercial liability insurance*—If the responsible driver was employed when he or she caused your accident, the employer is also liable and legally responsible for your injury claims. Most business policies carry high coverage limits. With significant money involved, these commercial insurance carriers employ the very best adjusters to oppose victim claims.

- *federal funding*—If your accident was caused by an agent of the federal government, the Federal Tort Claims Act abolishes sovereign immunity and allows claims against the federal government.

- ***state funding***—If a state employee or agency caused your accident, the state may be held liable under the North Carolina State Tort Claims Act. These claims are handled and defended by the state's attorney general. If a settlement cannot be reached, the case is tried and determined by the North Carolina Industrial Commission.

- ***uninsured motorist coverage***—If there is no liability insurance coverage for either the at-fault vehicle or the at-fault driver, the victim can collect injury claims payments through multiple sources of uninsured motorist (a.k.a. UM) coverage in his or her household. North Carolina allows stacking of UM policies. Thus, if you are the victim of an uninsured driver, you can collect from the uninsured motorist policy covering the vehicle you were riding in and also through other separate policies held by you and *every* other relative who resided with you on the accident date.

- ***underinsured motorist coverage***—If all liability insurance policies added together do not provide adequate funding to pay for your injury claims, you can collect additional benefits through multiple underinsured motorist (a.k.a. UIM) policies. Stacking of UIM policies is fully allowed in North Carolina. UIM coverage can be collected from the insurance policy for the vehicle you were riding in, your own policy if it is separate, and from all policies for *every* relative who resided with you on the date of accident.

These are the common sources of insurance coverage available to pay accident-related injury claims. For a complete list of all money sources available to pay accident victims, see chapter 1.

Proving and Collecting Medical Expenses: Billed Versus Paid—Tragic North Carolina Tort Reform

The rights of North Carolina accident victims are under attack. Recent legislation has dramatically decreased the value of personal injury cases in settlement and at trial. The new evidence law allows a jury to only see the amount of victim medical bills actually paid by health insurance. If the victim has no health insurance, the jury sees the full medical bill. If the victim has Medicaid or Medicare, doctors are forced to accept discounts of up to 85 percent of billed charges. For a victim with a $100,000.00 surgical bill paid by Medicaid, the jury is told that the total medical bill is only $15,000.00!

Insurance companies now insist that victims present medical bills along with proof of all health insurance payments. They then limit the amount they pay to the amount covered or paid by health insurance. Unfortunately, juries now only see part of the picture. They are told that the full medical bills are less than the actual amount charged by hospitals and doctors. This likely will result in very unfair verdicts. If billed treatment totaled $100,000.00, but a jury hears that total bills were only $15,000.00, they may conclude that treatment was less invasive and that injuries were less severe.

The task of presenting medical bills has been expanded because of the new law. The victim must now provide explanation of benefits (EOB) forms along with the raw medical bills to show exactly what was covered and paid by health insurance. If EOBs are not available, the victim must go to the doctor and demand invoices that show all payments, credits, and health insurance adjustments for all accident-related medical treatment.

Placing a Value on the Injury Case

It is impossible to provide a formula or list of reliable case values for various types of injuries. Victims of collision-related injury truly receive nothing more than a *cause of action*, or a mere right to sue. If another driver causes you injury, there is no formula or law that defines exactly what the other driver and all insurance carriers owe you. Instead, you are legally allowed to file a civil action and pursue a claim for all damages arising from driver negligence through a jury trial. If a jury grants a verdict in your favor, only then is the value of the case fixed. Until then, settlement negotiations are simply an effort to agree on what a jury might award.

Because of the nature of victims' legal claims, the only way to fairly value your personal injury claim is to research trial results and jury verdicts throughout the state of North Carolina. Focus primarily on your local area and counties that have similar demographic patterns and similar jury awards. Certain counties are typically more generous than others. Under the North Carolina Civil Practice Act, the plaintiff/victim can file suit in either his or her own county of residence or in the county where the defendant/at-fault driver resides. When researching case value, look at the most favorable available trial venue and price the claim in that county.

Online verdict research can be conducted using Lexis/Nexis and Westlaw accounts. The *North Carolina Verdict Reporter* is a printed publication that can be accessed through subscription. This is the most thorough catalogue of trial verdicts reached throughout the state in all types of civil cases. Also, the *Lawyer's Weekly* publication, which provides the most up-to-date reporting on the appellate decisions of the North Carolina Court of Appeals and the North Carolina Supreme Court, will also provide information about settlements and verdicts reached all over the state.

Proper determination of injury case value depends on careful consideration of the victim's unique circumstances and on the full impact of all injuries on the victim's life. There are certain value factors that are considered by insurance companies and by juries in the case value determination. Victims and lawyers should construct case presentations to highlight the following case value factors:

- ***driver error involved***—Egregious errors and intentional conduct typically lead to higher settlements and verdicts. For example, drunk driving or excessive speeding should increase settlement value.
- ***collision dynamics***—Head-on and roll-over collisions are the most frightening and dangerous. Care should be taken to highlight collision dynamics that would increase jury sympathy and awards.
- ***Driver-victim relationship***—If the victim is the guest passenger in the at-fault vehicle and if at-fault driver is a close friend or relative, the jury may be less inclined to render a large verdict. However, in some cases, the relationship increases case value. If the

at-fault driver is the defendant and a favorable witness on damages and the extent of suffering, the insurance carrier should tender a more generous payment.

- *emergency response*—Careful and proper description of the collision scene and emergency response can enhance case value. For example, if fire rescue is involved or if life flight is involved, we would always see higher verdicts and settlements. Similarly, victim entrapment and use of the Jaws of Life for extraction would also be a compelling and sympathetic fact warranting higher settlement value.

- *collision consequence evidence*—If the collision is particularly violent or horrific or if other victims suffered very serious injury, these factors would certainly be of interest to any jury. Be prepared to offer evidence that would help a jury distinguish more serious collisions from the fender-benders that typically occur.

- *victim collision scene experience*—If the victim is trapped in the vehicle and receiving medical attention at the scene or if he or she is forced to be placed under full spinal protocol at the scene, these factors would certainly increase victim anxiety and should be carefully described to insurance adjusters and jurors. The ambulance or life-flight experience and the details of hospital care should also be carefully described and considered.

- *timing of first medical attention*—Many collision victims are unaware of the extent of injury until twenty-four to forty-eight hours following the collision. While some victims are removed from the scene by ambulance or life flight, others may go directly home and later visit with physicians. Insurance companies always look at the timing of treatment. They perceive any delay as a suggestion that the injuries are minor or trivial.

- *nature of initial medical treatment*—If the collision results in ambulance transport, hospitalization, and emergency surgery, the case would certainly be more valuable than one involving more conservative injury and care.

- *nature and extent of follow-up treatment*—Please take your time to work with doctors until you have recovered from all injuries. Insurance adjusters always look at the nature and duration of medical care when they determine how much to pay for pain and suffering. An accident victim under medical care for two weeks would not receive as much compensation as the victim under medical care for six months. The nature and difficulty of medical care must also be considered. If medical care was primarily diagnostic testing, which revealed no injury, the award for pain and suffering would not be as high as for a victim with the same medical expense, where those expenses were for active clinical therapy and treatment.

- ***non-medical evidence of pain***—Medical records are typically the primary focus of adjusters and juries when determining the extent of the patient's pain. However, the patient's own testimony and testimony of friends and other witnesses also helps to establish the extent of the victim's physical pain and emotional suffering.

- ***victim's family situation***—If the injury and related limitations were particularly difficult because of the victim's lifestyle or responsibilities, the award for pain and suffering would higher. For example, a single mother who is rendered unable to work and care for her children would be entitled to more generous compensation because of her particular difficulties.

- ***amount of medical charges***—As noted in the "billed versus paid" discussion above, evidence of medical charges has been significantly restricted by recent North Carolina legislation. The total amount of medical bills is a key factor that insurance adjusters and juries typically rely on when determining how significant the injury truly was.

- ***extent of physical limitations and suffering***—Detailed care should be taken to interpret and summarize medical records to highlight all evidence confirming the patient's pain complaints and physical limitations. Juries today are most fair when their attention is focused on the extent of the patient's pain, limitations on mobility and physical ability, the impact of the injury on quality of life, and on the practical difficulties arising from personal injury.

- ***evidence of injury permanency***—Careful legal inquiries to physicians will generate the best and most thorough medical evidence confirming permanency of injury and the potential need for future medical care. Since the responsible driver owes for all medical treatment for the balance of the victim's life, thorough medical evidence must be offered to confirm all lasting symptoms, the likely prognosis and future course of all injuries, and the full cost of anticipated future medical treatment. Juries are typically quite generous with personal injury awards in cases involving permanent injury with significant physical limitation.

- *impact on employment and productivity*—Income loss claims must be supported by medical evidence that confirms that lost wages and missed work resulted from accident-related medical disability. If a physician orders the victim out of work, this allows the victim to collect all lost earnings. Juries also are typically more generous in the award of pain and suffering compensation when they see that a productive individual is forced to remain out of work.

- *quality of evidence of physical injury*—Photographs and video are the best evidence to show the extent of visible injuries and the course of healing. Take early steps to collect and preserve this evidence. It will generate significantly higher settlement offers and trial verdicts.

- *quality of legal representation and validity of trial threat*—If the insurance company sees that the victim has legal counsel with a reputation for successful trial practice in the personal injury arena, they will understand that they are fully obligated for your losses. They will see that if they do not offer a fair settlement, your lawyer will simply file suit and collect the same amount through a jury trial. If this occurs, they not only pay what they could have settled for, but they must also pay a lawyer to defend the at-fault driver in court, 8 percent prejudgment interest on your trial verdict, and their own medical experts.

- *extent of any scarring or disfigurement*—Permanently visible injuries result in higher settlements and trial verdicts. This is a relative value factor. A scar on a person's face is worth more than a scar on his or her foot. A scar on a younger individual is typically worth more than a scar on an older person. Scars on women are typically valued higher by juries than scars on men. Thus, we look at the extent of scarring and disfigurement uniquely based on the victim's age, gender, profession, and circumstances.

- ***personality of defendant***—If the at-fault driver is a drunk driver or is an otherwise unsavory character, this would typically result in a more generous trial verdict. If there are uniquely negative characteristics of the at-fault driver or the driver's conduct, this should increase case value.

- ***credibility and character of the victim***—The jury must like you and feel comfortable with you before they will grant a generous verdict. Evidence of past criminal convictions is often admissible as evidence of victim credibility. This seems terribly unfair, but it is the law. When determining whether to go to trial or whether you could expect a generous verdict, you should be honest about any prejudices the jury might have against you. Similarly, an honored or respected professional or otherwise likeable and credible victim would likely receive a more generous verdict from a jury.

Obviously, many factors are involved when a jury decides on the verdict and value of a personal injury claim. Therefore, many factors are involved in settlement negotiations and discussions with insurance carriers. Creative case presentation highlighting all positive value factors will certainly motivate higher settlement offers and more generous injury claim compensation. Take the time to creatively tell your story, and make sure that you convey the full impact that the collision and all related injuries have had on your life.

Injury Claim Settlement Process

Negotiating toward Settlement

If you are handling your case without counsel, please be aware that insurance adjusters will be offering less than they know your case would bring at trial. They take advantage of the fact that you are proceeding without legal advice and representation. They assume that you are interested settling, and they are not inclined to offer what you might win in court since they know you do not intend to go to court. They also assume that you are flying blind and that you do not have research and guidance confirming the true value of your injury claim in a trial setting. Considering these preconceptions, you must be prepared to lock horns with the adjuster to make sure that they truly hear your story, that they consider all evidence favorable to your side, and that they understand that you will hire counsel and proceed to trial if they do not pay a fair settlement.

Even skilled attorneys have to fight with insurance adjusters and insurance carriers to compel proper payment. Insurance companies always seek to limit their consideration of favorable evidence, and they always challenge the validity of all injury claims. They know that few victims truly want to go to court. Thus, they always test the victim with unfair, discounted offers. Rise to this challenge and file suit if a fair settlement offer is not tabled for your benefit.

After submission of the initial settlement demand and full case presentation, insurance adjusters will review your claims documentation and independently value your personal injury case. This process typically takes three to six weeks. After the initial demand is presented, the victim should patiently allow the insurance company to make the next move. If you appear to be in a hurry, your adjuster will assume that you are short on funds. Since the lawsuit process takes approximately twelve months, they know that the hurried victim in need of money now will not have the time to wait for a court date and fair verdict. Do not let any adjuster know that you are in financial difficulty. This will result in *severe* discounting of insurance settlement offers.

In most cases, the insurance company's initial offer is less than they will actually pay. They hold money back and seek to settle for the smallest possible amount. Be prepared to aggressively negotiate the injury claim. Stand ready with evidence of similar verdicts. Also, force the adjuster to acknowledge the medical evidence and demonstrate an understanding of the true impact of the injuries on your life. This is the *only* way to ensure that your offers are fair and proper. If the victim's payment demand and the insurance carrier's offer ultimately meet at an acceptable compromised figure, the case can be settled privately. If negotiation results in impasse, the only option for the victim is to conduct a trial and allow a jury to determine the true value of the injury case.

Settlement Versus Trial

Other than victims of drunk drivers, accident victims rarely have any interest in bringing their injury claim to trial. However, if the insurance carriers are not offering fair compensation, litigation and trial are the proper course to enforce your legal rights. Settlements are very simple. If you and the other side agree on case value, you sign a release and receive a check. The release is a contract wherein you accept an agreed-upon sum of money in exchange for your agreement to forfeit your right to file a lawsuit. Essentially, you are closing all claims and accepting the settlement amount as full and *final* payment for all injury-related damages.

Insurance regulations require an insurance carrier to fund a settled claim within ten days of the date of settlement. Thus, if you agree to a settlement amount, you can close your claim and secure payment within two weeks. Please be aware that the total amount of the settlement can be reduced after the release is signed by outside claims against your settlement. This issue is discussed in more detail later in this chapter. Before you agree to any settlement, make sure you understand where all of the settlement money is going. Be sure all medical bills are paid, and insist on disclosure of exactly how much net money you personally receive before you sign any release.

Chapter 7 provides information on the litigation and trial process. At this point, it is sufficient to note that litigation is a more time-consuming and expensive method of resolving the injury claim. However, most of the expenses fall to the insurance carriers and the other side. If your research or your attorneys suggest that the insurance carrier's offer is significantly less than the fair value of your injury case, you certainly should file suit and present your story at trial to twelve neighbors who live in your home county. Do not be afraid of court involvement or the trial process. Stand strong and enforce your rights to full and fair payment.

Injury Claim Settlement Documentation

If the injury case is settled between the victim and a single liability insurance carrier, the only document involved is a general release. Most injury claim releases are standard form releases. In the release, the defense does not acknowledge legal liability or fault. This is typical and safe language. Further, a proper release simply identifies the settlement amount and indicates that it is "a settlement of a claim of disputed amount and disputed legal liability." This language is safe and beneficial. If you reach a settlement without counsel, an attorney in the personal injury arena should be willing to review a release for you for a very small charge (if not free of charge entirely). Remember that a release closes your case and ends *all* potential future claims. Make sure that your health is recovered and that all expenses and losses are being honored before you sign away your rights.

If your settlement involves multiple at-fault parties or multiple insurance policies, there will be more than one release. If the claim is made against multiple liability insurance policies with no involvement of any underinsured motorist (UIM) coverage, then the case settlement would involve a single settlement with all liability payments being tendered simultaneously. You should not settle with one liable party or seek to separate your claims. Make sure all liable parties are at the table, and make sure the total payment is acceptable before reaching any verbal or written agreement. One release should be signed that identifies all parties involved in the settlement. If each liability insurer requests their own release, this is acceptable practice and all releases should be executed simultaneously.

If the settlement involves payment from Uninsured Motorist (UM) coverage, you must be certain that all available UM policies are involved in the settlement. Stacking of UM coverage allows an injury victim to collect from multiple UM sources. Since the individual policies and insurers have shared, proportionate liability, you must involve all carriers and adjusters in the settlement. Typically, each carrier will ask that their own release be signed. In a UM case, the release is unique and does not release the at-fault driver and other liable parties. Rather, it releases the insurance carrier from further obligations under the policy that provides UM coverage. In addition, the UM carrier will typically ask the claimant to sign a subrogation agreement containing the claimant's agreement to cooperate if the UM insurance carrier decides to pursue the uninsured driver for reimbursement.

If the claim involves payment from liability insurance and also from UIM, the settlement may be reached in two stages. The first stage is the liability settlement. Here, the claimant must confirm with certainty that *all* liable parties are identified and that all liability insurance policies are involved in settlement talks. If all liability coverage is offered, the victim must then secure written confirmation from the liability insurance carriers that the total amount of available liability coverage is being offered, tendered, and exhausted. This "written liability tender" is provided to the UIM insurers (all stackable policies must be involved at this stage), and they have thirty days from receipt of the liability tender notice to determine whether they wish to subrogate against any at-fault parties. Here, the UIM insurance carriers are looking at the wealth and assets of all responsible parties to determine whether they want to file suit after settlement with the victim to seek reimbursement of any amount they pay in UIM benefits. Before the end of the thirty-day period, the UIM insurer must pay the amount of the liability tender offer to the claimant if they wish to preserve their right to seek reimbursement from any at-fault parties. This payment is called a *UIM advance*, and the effect is to pay over the liability coverage amount to the victim while, at the same time, preventing the victim from signing any type of release or covenant in favor of the at-fault parties.

In most UIM cases, the UIM insurer will not pay the UIM advance and they will not preserve their rights to subrogation and reimbursement. In these cases, the settlement is reached in two stages. In the first stage, the victim settles with the liability insurance carrier by signing a *covenant not to enforce judgment* (hereinafter referred to as a "covenant"). The covenant contains the victim's promise that he or she will not seek any money or assets from the at-fault party. The legal effect is to preserve the victim's rights to payment under all available UIM policies and to allow the victim to bring the case through trial if necessary to determine case value and to force payment from UIM carriers. However, the covenant also provides that if the trial verdict exceeds the amount of available UIM coverage, the victim cannot collect any amount directly from the at-fault parties or seek payment of any amount that exceeds the available UIM coverage.

If your claim involves serious injuries and large money damages, and if you are facing a liability limits tender with additional benefits available through UIM policies, proceed with tremendous caution. Secure independent asset searches to confirm the wealth and assets of all responsible parties. If your case is worth more than the total of all UIM coverage/policies available, you should pause before signing a covenant. If the responsible parties have the ability to pay, you may prefer to forego early settlement opportunities and instead proceed to trial to secure a verdict and judgment. Following trial, you would have the right to collect immediately from all liability and UIM insurance sources and to also immediately seek additional payment by enforcing your judgment against all named defendants.

If you prefer to settle your injury claims at or below the total amount of insurance coverage available under all liability and UIM coverage sources, then you can settle the case involving liability and UIM in two stages as follows: first, you secure a liability limits tender and then provide written notice of liability tender to all UIM insurance carriers. The UIM insurers have thirty days to decide whether they will preserve their right to subrogation by paying the amount of the liability tender offer through a UIM advance payment or if they will waive their subrogation rights and allow the victim to settle directly with the liability insurance carrier. If they waive subrogation, the victim will sign a covenant and then receive the liability limits payment. Thereafter, the victim must present medical evidence and settlement demands to all UIM carriers and push toward a second payment through settlement with all UIM adjusters. If settlement can be reached, the UIM carriers will seek signatures on a UIM release, which contains the victim's agreement that he or she can present no further claims against that policy.

Some insurance companies are adding Medicare hold harmless agreements to their settlement documents. Medicare has rapidly changing rights to share in injury settlement proceeds. If you expect to become eligible for Medicare or Social Security benefits within the thirty-month period following settlement, Medicare has potential rights to reach back and demand part of your settlement money.

Medicare rights are beyond the scope of this text. At settlement, you should determine whether Medicare paid any medical bills for you and also determine what rights they might have in your case. If Medicare paid some of your medical charges, they will provide their lien claim amount in writing or through their online portal. This lien must be paid. Holding the amount from settlement and paying promptly will protect Medicare's interest. Thus, the hold harmless agreement is of no consequence. Most insurers currently will allow a claimant to refuse signature on the hold harmless provision and complete the settlement with only a general release. Try this approach and seek legal advice if you must sign a Medicare hold harmless agreement.

If you are represented by counsel, your attorney should handle all paperwork and settlement documentation for your benefit. Attorneys should also provide a thorough accounting of how all settlement monies will be collected and disbursed *before* you agree to this settlement and sign the release.

The Vanishing Settlement

Outside Claims against Settlement Proceeds

Injury law has become far more complicated in recent years. Recent federal and state law changes have allowed health insurance companies and doctors to level financial claims directly against your personal injury settlement proceeds. If you do not have an attorney, insurance adjusters will typically pay these outside claims in full. They do not take steps to negotiate these claims down or to avoid these claims when they are not valid liens or settlement reductions.

Insurance adjusters are only worried about closing their case, and they are not willing to risk later financial obligations. Thus, they may settle your case for a promised amount, have you sign a release, and then hand your money over to doctors or health insurance companies. Before you agree to a settlement in private dealings with insurance companies, make sure that they have your net settlement check in hand. Also, have them carefully itemize all intended payments from settlement proceeds. You should know exactly where the settlement money is going *before* you agree to the lump-sum settlement and sign any release.

Attorneys increase client settlement proceeds by negotiating for the highest possible injury claim settlement *and then* by protecting your settlement from outside claims. The best personal injury attorneys make a huge impact on the victim's bottom line payment by carefully confronting every outside claim against the victim's settlement. Most victims are concerned with the exact amount of money they personally receive. A large settlement may be less desirable if most of the money will go to the victim's health insurance carrier and then to pay unpaid medical charges or to reimburse employer's short-term disability and long-term disability benefits plans. You or your attorney should investigate all of these outside claims, confirm the validity of each claim, refuse payment of invalid claims, negotiate reductions in valid claims, and thereby increase the net amount of money you receive at the close of the injury case.

The most common outside claims against injury claim money are as follows:

- *Unpaid medical bills*—Under N.C.G.S. 44-49 and 44-50, hospitals and other medical providers have a right to direct payment of at least some portion of unpaid medical bills from any insurance money paid to the injury victim.
- *ERISA qualified health insurance plan*—Most health insurance carriers have a right to be paid back when they pay health insurance

benefits to cover accident-related medical bills. These liens can take the entire settlement.

- *Medicare liens*—Medicare currently has several proposals that may increase their liens against settlement money. Medicare liens must be dealt with to avoid loss of future Medicare or Social Security benefits.

- *Medicaid liens*—Medicaid's lien currently cannot take the entire settlement. Recent legislative proposals threaten to change this rule. Medicaid's liens must be scrutinized to remove unrelated medical charges.

- *Child support liens*—Unpaid child support can be claimed directly from settlement money if the child support enforcement representative learns of the settlement and notifies the adjuster or the attorney.

- *Disability income benefit liens*—If an employer-provided disability plan is qualified under the federal ERISA statutes, the disability insurer has a legal right to be paid back some portion of the benefits from the injury settlement.

- *Veterans Administration liens*—The VA provides health care to veterans at no charge. If they provide accident-related care, they will calculate medical charges and seek payment from an injury settlement.

- *Vocational rehabilitation liens*—If a local vocational rehab or social services organization provides health care or assistance to an accident victim, they are allowed to ask for payment for these services from settlement funds.

- *Workers' compensation liens*—If the victim was working when the accident occurred, workers' comp will pay for all medical care, lost wages, and other benefits. They have strong rights to collect from the injury settlement, and they can even retain counsel to take control of the victim's case. Their claims should be carefully scrutinized. Discounts can be negotiated, and in some cases, the lien can be judicially waived by the court. The injured employee should avoid overpayment of workers' comp liens.

Taxes on the Injury Settlement

Under the Internal Revenue Code, payment to an accident victim made for pain, injury, and suffering is nontaxable. Because the tax code is constantly changing and because there are certain exceptions to this general rule, you should consult your accountant and tax advisors to determine the tax effect of your settlement. However, you should be hopeful because in almost every case, there is no state or federal income tax due from your injury settlement!

The only concern and primary exception to the non-tax rule is the case where money is collected for lost income. If you collect a specific amount for lost wages, this compensation would be subject to income tax. However, most settlements are structured as "lump sum" settlements, and the claim is also identified as "disputed" in nature and amount. As long as a specific amount is not collected or identified in the Release documents as lost wage reimbursement, the entire settlement should be shielded from income tax obligations. Your personal injury attorney or tax advisors can help you consider your case and your financial circumstances to be certain that you do not have to share your settlement money with state or federal tax authorities.

CHAPTER 6

❖

COMMON TRAUMATIC INJURIES

Evidence and Case Value Considerations

Truly great personal injury lawyers have as much knowledge and experience in the fields of anatomy and medicine as they do in the fields of law and trial practice. Legal dominance and leverage is best applied with thorough medical expertise. Insurance companies always seek to minimize or trivialize victims' injuries. To overcome the defense, medical evidence must be developed and utilized to *prove* the full extent of all injuries. Skilled physicians must be involved to show the relationship between the collision and the injuries, the full cost of all past and future care, and the likely course of future pain and medical problems that will remain over the full span of the victim's life. This approach is the only path toward securing full compensation in a serious injury case.

Claims adjusters receive very little medical training. They use their limited medical knowledge only to cherry-pick medical records and conversations with the victim to find weaknesses in the claim. They look at pre-accident medical records to argue that the injury is a "preexisting condition." They pull and highlight only those medical notes where the victim reports "mild" or "slight" pain. They look for missed appointments and "gaps in treatment." They *never* dig beneath the surface to explore the true severity of your injuries or to consider the potential permanent effects of your injuries.

To collect fair payment for serious injury, which is money you truly may need for health reasons later, you must demonstrate superior medical knowledge and provide thorough medical evidence to prove all negative impacts that the collision imposed on your quality of life. In this chapter, we explore medical and legal issues relating to the most common traumatic injuries arising from motor vehicle or pedestrian accidents. Every injury victim should analyze and research his or her injuries and carefully develop medical evidence to compel full and fair payment on all personal injury claims. When multiple injuries exist, care should be taken to show the overlay of multiple injuries and the cumulative effect of all injuries on the victim's health, abilities, and quality of life.

The following are the most common injuries confronted by pedestrians, bicyclists, motorcyclists, and drivers involved in roadway collisions.

Abrasions and Lacerations

Abrasions range in severity depending on the extent and depth of skin damage. Motorcycle collisions often result in very serious, large abrasions commonly referred to as *road rash*. Because abrasions involve damage to large surface areas of the skin, sutures and staples are typically not appropriate. Treatment for large abrasions is similar to care provided for burn injuries. In more severe cases, skin grafting is necessary. Here, the graft site (commonly the patient's thigh) will be a secondary wound site presented as part of the injury claim.

Lacerations are deep cuts to the skin, which range in severity depending on the depth and length of the cut. Butterfly bandaging will be used to close less serious lacerations. For deep lacerations, sutures and staples are commonly utilized for closure. In some cases, infection results in significant worsening of the laceration. Antibiotics, corrective surgery, wound drains, and other aggressive treatment is typically required to arrest infection and promote proper healing.

Scarring and Disfigurement

Disfigurement is a change to the structure and visible appearance of the body. Examples include cases of amputation or paralysis. Severe fracture and ligament injuries can also leave visibly apparent limited use of limbs or body parts.

Juries are most generous when injury results in obvious deformity for the victim. In these cases, the medical presentation should be very detailed and must include testimony confirming the patient's prognosis. Also, a functional capacity evaluation should be conducted by a physiatrist, a skilled orthopedic surgeon, or other relevant specialist to show with certainty how the deformity will limit physical ability, earning capacity, and quality of life. The case presentation should also provide a careful analysis of the victim's hobbies and activities before the accident, and the limiting effect of injuries on the victim's post-accident work duties, hobbies, travels, and day-to-day activities.

Scarring is a more limited type of deformity. Scars can arise from the initial traumatic injury or from subsequent surgery. Most scars also involve nerve damage, which can cause itching, pain, or numbness. Neurologists typically agree, after a two-year healing period, that any lingering nerve damage symptoms will be permanent.

Plastic surgeons have numerous techniques to reduce the appearance of scarring. The two most common approaches are dermabrasion and excision. Dermabrasion involves the use of course emollients to scour away the surface scar and all surrounding tissue. Thereafter, the entire region heals uniformly, which decreases the relative appearance of the scar.

Excision is a local surgical approach whereby the scar is cleanly and carefully cut away. Thereafter, the surgeon uses microsutures to bring the healthy tissue surrounding the scar together, creating a much finer and cleaner wound. Following excision, most scars remain visible but they are far less obvious.

In cases involving permanent scarring, photographs should be presented to support the injury claim. Ideally a series of photos will be offered to show the condition of the wound immediately after the accident, the wound with sutures or staples in place, the condition of the wound during the healing process, and the current scar appearance. The victim should also provide testimony concerning the emotional effect of scarring and any other limitations that the scar has caused.

Scarring cases are often defended by insurance carriers by utilizing social media evidence to suggest that the victim is not bothered by the scar. Adjusters cull the web for Facebook entries and other open-access social media. If the victim claims that the scar causes embarrassment or reduced physical ability, contrary online entries are often presented by the defense. For example, if a young lady suggests she never wears short sleeves due to the appearance of arm scars, the defense seeks to show online photos of the victim depicting brief moments where the scar is visible and the victim appears happy. Accident victims should always restrict their online presence to avoid their Facebook, Twitter, or other web entries and photos being taken out of context by insurance adjusters.

Fractures—Broken Bone Cases

The medical term for a broken bone is a *fracture*. Many factors must be considered to determine the severity of a fracture and the proper medical approach to treatment. Generally speaking, there are twelve types of fractures diagnosed by physicians:

1. *Avulsion Fracture*—Ligaments connect muscle to bone at the joint and the ligament motivates joint movement with muscle contraction. An avulsion fracture occurs when the ligament is pulled away from its anchor to the bone such that the bone is cracked or broken through.
2. *Comminuted Fracture*—These are more severe fractures where the bone is broken in more than two places or is broken into fragments.
3. *Complete Fracture*—The bone has cleanly broken into two pieces.

4. ***Compression Fracture***—This break is caused when the structure of the bone collapses, typically under traumatic force and sudden pressure.
5. ***Greenstick Fracture***—An incomplete fracture typically caused by twisting of the bone resulting in a small and narrow crack on one side of the bone.
6. ***Hairline Fracture***—A slight/minimal break in the bone with no significant bone displacement or damage.
7. ***Impacted Fracture***—The edge of two bones become wedged together by traumatic force.
8. ***Oblique Fracture***—The bone breaks at an angle and the fracture extends across the length of the structure of the bone.
9. ***Spiral Fracture***—The break involved in a severe twisting injury has a spiral or corkscrew-like appearance across the surface/shaft of the bone.
10. ***Stress Fracture***—Small cracks or hairline fractures in the bones arising from sports, heavy activity, repetitive trauma, and overuse.
11. ***Transverse Fracture***—A break straight across the affected bone.
12. ***Intra-Articular Fracture***—A break in the bones that occurs across the pivotal section of a joint and affects the function of the joint.

Treatment of the fracture will depend on the location and severity of the bone damage. An intra-articular fracture is a fracture across the midline of a joint. These injuries often require surgical intervention and repair, and orthopedic hardware is commonly used to stabilize and repair the fracture. In such cases, a high risk of arthritic changes exists for the patient. Osteolysis (disintegration or degradation of the bone) can also occur where screws or fasteners attach plates to bones. Careful attention must be given to the potential costs involved for future surgery to repair or remove orthopedic hardware. Also, long-term care needs, including arthritis medication and other pain management, should be considered in every serious fracture case. The victim deserves compensation to cover all potential future medical needs.

Growth-plate fractures in children also require careful medical and legal consideration. Fractured bones in children present long-term implications because their bones are still growing and have not fully matured. Until this process is complete, a child's bones continue to expand in length and shape at the area near the ends of the long bones. This region is called the *growth plate*, or *physis*.

The growth plate is the weakest part of the child's skeleton. Thus, an injury to a growing child's joint is more likely to cause harm to the bone's growth plate than to the surrounding ligaments and connective tissues. In these cases, the child's bones may grow unequally after the fracture so that the injured leg or arm may grow to a different length than the unaffected limb. Growth-plate fractures make up 15 percent of all fractures in children. Always look at the potential long-term effects of joint and growth-plate fractures when considering the fair value of a minor child's personal injury claim.

When presenting an injury claim involving a broken bone, the case presentation should carefully demonstrate the location and extent of all fractures. Medical diagrams are excellent tools to graphically show the steps involved in the complicated surgeries conducted by orthopedic surgeons. X-rays should also be provided with the demand brochure to show pre-repair and post-surgical appearance of the fracture. A negative image of the X-ray (which is itself a film negative) can be created to best show the detailed condition of the injured bones and the placement and presence of plates/screws/rods and other hardware. Orthopedic narrative reports help to prove the full extent of the fracture, the severity of all symptoms and physical limitations, permanency of injury, and all potential future medical problems the fracture might impose. A life care plan may also be necessary to prove the cost of future medical treatment needed by the patient. If multiple fractures arise from a single accident, the cumulative effects of all injuries must be shown to motivate proper payment for the victim's pain and suffering.

Brain, Spinal Cord, and Nervous System Injuries

Neuroanatomy is the most complex and rapidly evolving field in medicine. Trauma to the brain can cause lasting and occasionally debilitating symptoms including headaches, blurred vision, memory loss, speech and communicative impairment, hearing loss or tinnitus (ringing in the ears), vertigo, dizziness, sleep loss, agitation, mood swings, and in more severe cases, coma or fatality. Traumatic brain injury (TBI) is a specialized focus for doctors and attorneys. In some cases, concussion causes persistent symptoms resulting in a diagnosis of post-concussive syndrome. Also, diffuse organic brain damage can occur due to blunt force trauma to the head or severe shaking sufficient to cause collision between the brain and the interior of the cranium.

It is very difficult to properly diagnose and quantify traumatic brain injuries. Neuropsychologists have developed many tests that help to objectively document the extent of memory loss and loss of cognitive and functional impairment. New treatment options are constantly arising in this field, and there is wonderful hope for patients with brain injuries.

The most frightening head injuries involve intracranial hemorrhage. If bleeding occurs below the surface of the skull, this can result in severe and permanent brain damage for the patient. Typically, emergency surgery is performed to open the cranium and release internal pressure and bleeding. After repairs are made to arrest bleeding, draining devices are installed to equalize and maintain proper intracranial pressure.

TBI patients are often unable to return home due to their injuries. They require inpatient care at skilled nursing care facilities. The injury case must show all medical and life-care costs that the patient will expect over the full balance of his or her life to ensure that the funds recovered are sufficient to allow access to cutting-edge medical options and to provide every possible comfort to the victim.

Injuries to the nerves of the spine can also cause devastating loss of function for the patient. Spinal cord injuries vary in severity depending upon location, with injuries at higher levels of the spine being the most severe. Injuries to the spinal cord are classified as partial or complete. If the injury is "complete," the victim will have no mobility, feeling, or function of the body below the point of injury. With a partial injury to the spinal cord, the person may be able to partially move one limb or perhaps have more use of one side of the body than the other.

Spinal cord injuries to the neck and cervical spine frequently result in quadriplegia. Injuries above the level of the fourth cervical vertebra (C4) may require use of a ventilator to allow the patient to breathe. Injury to C5 causes a loss of control at the wrist and hand, but the victim can still use his or her shoulder. Trauma to the C6 vertebra typically results in the loss hand function. Injuries at C2 are often the most profound. Christopher Reeve, the famous actor who suffered severe injury due to a horseback riding accident, endured his injury at this level of his cervical spine.

In spinal cord injury cases, it is often difficult to show a jury the extent of disability and discomfort in a trial setting. The victim should be present for some part of the trial, if possible. However, it is typically best not to force an uncomfortable, ongoing presence, and therefore, family members may sit in at the plaintiff's table during the trial. Where the victim cannot physically tolerate the full trial and during medication and settlement negotiations, it is best to secure a day-in-the-life video to show how the injury has truly impacted day-to-day quality of life. Vendors provide videography services and a quality documentary can typically be professionally produced at a reasonable cost. This evidence is essential to force insurance carriers, responsible parties, and a jury to truly consider the extent of pain, disfigurement, immobility, and disability imposed by the spinal injury. Family members should also be encouraged to secure photographs, video, and other evidence (e.g., diaries) during the healing process to help secure proof of the devastating difficulties produced by these injuries.

Back Injury

Back injuries are the most common injuries seen in motor vehicle accident cases. Frankly, back injuries are also the most common target for those who pretend to be injured and present fraudulent claims. This unfortunate reality makes it far more difficult for the true victim of a back injury to be fairly heard.

Back pain is a common and major health problem that extracts an enormous emotional and financial toll on the patient. Eighty percent of the population experiences back pain during their lifetime, and back pain is the second leading cause of missed time from work in the United States. While back pain can occur without trauma, traumatic injury to the spine can cause very severe and debilitating pain with symptoms radiating into all extremities.

The spine is actually a series of joints. The vertebrae are the small bones that align one on top of the other and extend from the base of the skull to the bottom of the pelvis. There are seven bones in the cervical spine, typically labeled C1 through C7. There are twelve bones in the thoracic spine, labeled T1 through T12. There are five bones in the lumbar spine, labeled L1 through L5. There are five fused bones that make up the sacrum, labeled S1 through S5. The coccyx or tailbone is a structure composed of four fused bones located at the very base of the spine.

In between each two adjacent vertebrae, a soft-tissue pad exists to separate the vertebrae, to cushion the joint, and to facilitate joint motion. Injury to this pad is commonly called a "disc injury." The medical term for this pad or disc is a *nucleus pulposa*.

Trauma to the spine can result in damage to the spinal ligaments, connective tissues, surrounding muscle structure, or the bones or discs. Disc damage can range in symptomology from mild to severe and from temporary to permanent. Because the nerves of the spine pass through openings in the vertebrae along the range of the patient's back, damage to the vertebrae or discs can cause stenosis, which is a narrowing or squeezing of the joint space where the nerves reside.

In some spinal injury cases, symptoms are not immediately perceived by the victim. This is because nerve involvement is often progressive and can occur and increase over time. These injuries are often latent, meaning they are symptomatically dormant for some period of time. Thus, you may be dealing with a very serious spinal injury that has not yet presented pain or other symptoms. If your collision involves significant force and/

or speed, it is wise to be carefully diagnosed and evaluated for spinal injuries.

Damage to the intervertebral disc / nucleus pulposa is typically of three varieties and can also occur as a combination of all three types:

1. *Bulging Disc*—A bulging or slipped disc occurs when the nucleus pulposa is pushed out of the normal location such that it extrudes beyond the perimeter of the adjacent vertebral surface. If the bulging disc extrudes rearward into the nerve passage, this can impinge the nerve, causing significant pain and limitation.
2. *Ruptured or Herniated Disc*—The nucleus pulposa consists of a multilayered outer skin, called the annulus, and protein pulp contained within the annulus. If the annulus is torn, allowing the disc contents to escape, this is called a ruptured disc, herniated disc, or herniated nucleus pulposa. This condition often requires surgery to replace the disc with a prosthetic pad or to remove the disc and fuse the surrounding vertebrae. This is a very serious condition requiring careful medical and legal consideration of all past and future treatment costs and physical consequences.
3. *Torn Annulus*—If the skin of the disc is partially torn but the protein pulp is not freed from the annulus, this injury is called a torn annulus. These injuries can be difficult to diagnose but are the common source of very severe back pain arising from trauma.

Fractures to the vertebrae are also common in collision cases. The medical response and the severity of the injury typically depend on the location of the fracture, the extent that the fracture affects the anatomy and function of the bone, and the number of vertebrae involved. Orthopedic surgeons and neurologists are often involved in the care and treatment of these injuries.

Whiplash injuries typically refer to injuries that do not involve vertebral fracture. In most of these cases, the primary damage is to the muscles, ligaments, and connective tissue around the spine. These injuries are complex and difficult to treat. For some patients, the effects of whiplash can last a lifetime. Chiropractors, orthopedic doctors, and physical therapists are most commonly involved in the treatment of these injuries.

In all back injury cases, insurance companies always look at the patient's history of prior complaints. They also will commonly place unfair weight on any degenerative findings in X-rays, MRI and CT imaging, and in other medical notes and diagnostic reports. Do not allow your adjuster to deny your back injury claims on grounds that there is evidence of degeneration. *Every* individual aged thirty or older is properly classified and diagnosed as having "degenerative disc disease." Simply put, all of us experience degeneration in the spine at and after age thirty. Patients with severe degeneration, such as cases involving osteophytes (bone spurs), severe arthritis, spondylosis (disease process of the bone that occurs over time), scoliosis (improper curvature of the spine), and other similar conditions would have more difficulty proving that their back injury was caused by the collision. However, even if you had back pain and problems before an accident, the responsible parties certainly owe for any worsening of your condition. Careful legal steps must be taken to organize and present all medical evidence to properly prove the impact of the collision on spinal health.

Facial Injuries

Most collision-related facial injuries result from air bag deployment. Airbag burns to the face and neck can be quite severe and painful. However, these injuries are transient and far less severe than a direct impact to the steering wheel, dash panel, or windshield.

Significant facial trauma can result in lacerations with sutures to the outside of the face or the inside of the mouth. A severe head strike can also result in a fracture to the nose and sinus bones, fracture to the jaw or teeth, fracture to the eye orbit or skull. Emergency care protocol calls for cranial CT scans in head trauma cases. These scans and X-ray radiological studies will reveal the extent of facial fractures. In more serious cases, surgery is required to repair orbital fractures, nasal fractures, and jaw fractures.

Injuries to the head and face often motivate very high jury awards. In settlement talks, the victim should present detailed medical evidence and photographs to show exactly how the injuries occurred and how the facial injuries appeared during the first weeks following the collision. X-rays and other graphic evidence, including medical diagrams showing any surgical processes, should be part of the claim presentation. Current photos should be offered along with reports from plastic surgeons to document permanency of scarring and any nerve damage or other lasting symptoms. In some cases, nerve pain medicine (e.g., gabapentin) will be used to reduce nerve pain associated with facial scars. If this is a permanent need for the patient, the full cost of this expensive medicine should be collected to fund all pain management needs over the balance of the patient's life.

In facial injury cases involving fracture, the victim must present very detailed medical reports and evidence to prove the future effects of these injuries. If fracture occurs to the jaw, associated problems, such as dental alignment and traumatic TMJ, should be considered and fully addressed by a maxillofacial surgeon. If fracture occurs near the eye orbit, careful consideration by medical specialists should be undertaken to prove any future problems that might arise relating to vision, optic nerve damage, or eye alignment. Finally, nasal fractures should also be carefully analyzed to isolate proof of any permanent breathing difficulties or any potential need for future nasal surgery.

Facial injuries resulting in permanent scarring or disfigurement should bring generous compensation for pain and suffering. Emotional injury should be carefully documented, and the victim's gender, age, profession, and other considerations should be addressed in the injury case presentation. Care should also be taken to consider Facebook and other social media entries to ensure that the claims of emotional injury cannot be impeached with open-access social media entries depicting the victim in a context that suggests a lack of emotional discomfort with facial scarring.

Dental/Tooth Injuries

Injuries to the teeth are common in collision cases. Whether by direct impact or by bite-down damage, the teeth can easily be loosened or fractured in an accident. To understand the nature of damage to the teeth, we must first consider dental terminology, the characteristics of teeth, and their relationship to the tissue and bones of the mouth.

Periodontal tissue is the delicate tissue that covers the bones inside the mouth. This tissue is integral in supporting and maintaining the teeth in the oral cavity. Wounds inside the mouth are very intricate and difficult to repair. Fortunately, this tissue is quick to heal and, while these injuries are painful, tissue repairs are typically effective toward a full recovery. Periodontal tissue is integral in supporting and maintaining the teeth in the oral cavity. The teeth are anchored into the bones of the mouth by periodontal ligaments. These ligaments allow for slight movement of the teeth within the bones and are sensitive to the pressure applied to the teeth. Severe damage to periodontal ligaments will result in loss to the affected teeth.

Two arches form the shape of the mouth: the maxillary arch and the mandibular arch. The maxillary arch is the front portion of the skull that forms the upper jaw, which holds the upper teeth in place. The maxillary arch also connects to the left and right cheeks, or zygomatic bones.

The mandibular arch is made up of the mandible or lower jawbone. This bone is the largest bone in the face and holds the lower teeth in place. Damage to either primary arch typically requires surgery. This damage also can cause permanent damage to the teeth.

Most collision-related dental injuries are to the central incisors and lateral incisors. These are the frontmost teeth. Although all teeth differ in size and shape, their basic structure is the same. There are three primary parts of a tooth: the crown, the neck, and the root. The crown is the part of the tooth visible above the gum line. The neck of the tooth is a constriction separating the crown from the root of the tooth. The root is the invisible portion of the tooth below the gum line that anchors the tooth into the jaw.

Tooth damage ranges in severity depending on the extent of the surface fracture and the extent of effect on the pulp, which lines each tooth. The pulp is a combination of living tissue, nerves, and blood that nourishes and provides sensation to the tooth's structure. If damage extends only to the enamel, which is the outer visible surface of the tooth, repairs are typically simple and cosmetic in nature. If damage reaches the inner layer (called the dentin) or exposes the pulp, removal or replacement of the tooth is typically necessary.

Dental injuries are permanent injuries and most repairs will not last the patient's lifetime. Attorneys and victims must always secure narrative opinions from the dentist, oral surgeon, or orthodontist to confirm the likely future treatment needs of the patient over the course of his or her remaining life span. These charges should be paid at settlement by all of the parties and insurance carriers that are responsible for the victim's injuries. Also the anxiety and pain associated with root canals, tooth removal, facial surgery, and other invasive dental treatment should be highlighted to secure proper compensation for pain and suffering.

Chest Injuries

Chest trauma caused by seat-belt tension or blunt-force trauma can be extremely painful and occasionally life threatening. The bones of the chest include the sternum (or breastbone) and the ribs, which articulate from the sternum and surround the organs of the chest. Sternum fractures can be extremely painful. If the fracture is not comminuted or displaced, little can be done medically for the patient. Only time and rest will heal these injuries. Thus, we see relatively little medical treatment and small medical expenses even though the pain from these injuries is quite severe. The attorney or victim should present medical research to demonstrate the extent of disability and pain arising from these injuries. Claims adjusters frequently look first at the amount of medical charges when considering the fair amount to be paid for pain and suffering. Because little medical expense arises from these very painful injuries, you must aggressively present medical evidence and anecdotal evidence to highlight the true impact of blunt-force chest trauma.

Physicians also typically do not aggressively treat rib fractures. In fact, X-ray studies in the emergency department are typically a short series and will not reveal all rib fractures. Hospital physicians are mainly looking for organ damage and evidence of displaced rib fractures. If the ribs are not separated or fragmented, current medical protocol is to provide no treatment other than activity restrictions and pain medication.

Chest trauma also frequently results in pneumothorax or collapsed lung. Damage to the lungs and lung tissue can be extremely dangerous. Collapsed lungs can negatively affect respiration and oxygenation for the patient, and more serious pneumothorax cases can produce permanent pulmonary damage. Symptoms of collapsed lung include difficulty breathing and pain. If the pneumothorax is left untreated, the patient can transition quickly from respiratory distress to shock. Pneumothorax can be diagnosed by the absence of breath sounds or by plain-film X-ray. The X-ray will confirm an accumulation of air outside of the lungs.

Treatment of pneumothorax requires the physicians to restore the normal pressure within the chest cavity. This is done by inserting a tube into the chest wall to allow the displaced air to escape. The chest tube will remain in place for several days to make sure the lung has not only correctly reinflated but also remains properly inflated.

A hemothorax is similar to a pneumothorax except it represents an accumulation of blood instead of air within the chest cavity. This condition is usually the result of a broken rib that punctures the lung. Treatment again involves the insertion of a chest tube to remove accumulated blood and restore proper respiratory function. A "sucking chest wound" is a more serious injury involving a puncture of the chest wall that allows air to pass in and out of the chest with each breath. This condition, also known as an open pneumothorax, requires the external wound to be sealed.

Another common blunt-force chest injury is a pericardial tamponade. The heart is surrounded by a sack known as the pericardium. Pericardial tamponade occurs when blood or fluid collects within the pericardium. This fluid and pressure prevents the heart from expanding properly, thereby restricting its pumping action. This condition is typically caused by a penetrating chest injury, but it can also occur in blunt chest trauma resulting in a myocardial rupture or an aortic tear. These are extremely serious and life-threatening injuries that typically result in emergency cardiac surgery to rescue the patient.

Pulmonary contusions or bruised lungs are also common in vehicle collisions. A bruised lung is the by-product of trauma to the lung tissue, which causes blood and fluid to accumulate in the tiny air sacs of the lungs. This condition can cause breathing difficulties and sometimes progresses into a condition called acute respiratory distress syndrome (ARDS). Motor vehicle collisions involving rapid deceleration (immediate stop due to collision impact force) are the single most common cause of pulmonary contusions.

Traumatic tears to the aorta are perhaps the most frightening and dangerous injuries resulting from blunt-force chest trauma. The aorta is the major artery that carries oxygenated blood from the heart to the other arteries and areas of the body. An aortal tear is a lethal injury that carries an 80 percent prehospital mortality rate. Up to 15 percent of all auto-accident-related deaths result from injury to the aorta. This large artery is most vulnerable to injury from frontal or side impacts.

Abdominal Injury

Abdominal trauma can occur because of sudden tightening of the lap belt or other blunt-force trauma caused by collision. Injuries to the intestines or internal organs are extremely dangerous and sometimes lethal. Lacerations to the spleen, liver, or kidneys can have profound impact on the patient's future health. Careful medical research should be performed on a case-by-case basis to illustrate the likely future effect of abdominal injury for the patient. Claims adjusters typically treat these as transient conditions that are frightening at first but result in a full recovery. If medical evidence indicates otherwise, legal leverage should be applied to enforce full rights of compensation.

Clavicle/Collarbone Injury

Clavicle injuries can be very complicated, and they are quite common in motor vehicle accidents. Collarbone fractures are particularly common in pedestrian accidents, bicycle accidents, and motorcycle accidents. The collarbone is a relatively weak bone and will fracture with fifteen pounds of sudden traumatic force. A clavicle fracture is properly characterized as a chest injury. However, the clavicle articulates from the sternum to the shoulder, and because injury to this bone is quite common, we consider these injuries separately.

In cases involving hairline fracture or non-displaced fracture, inactivity and proper splinting are often sufficient to promote a full recovery. However, if the collarbone is broken into separate pieces, repair and recovery can be extremely complicated. The obvious symptom of a displaced, nonunion fracture would be significant dropping of the shoulder and arm. A figure-eight brace loops under the arm and also around the neck and is used to apply pressure to the underside of the arm, pulling it upward toward the patient's neck. In my experience, physicians may rely on bracing too often in displaced fracture cases. The more certain repair would be surgery either to the repair the bone from the outside with a plate and screws or from the inside with a rod that is later removed once the bone heals sufficiently and in proper anatomic alignment.

If a displaced collarbone fracture is not surgically repaired, the bones occasionally will not properly rejoin. Instead, a fibrous union develops between the bones, creating a "false joint." With this healing, there is a hinge point in the shaft of the clavicle, allowing movement that would otherwise be prevented by the collarbone. In all clavicle fracture cases, careful diagnostic studies should be undertaken for the entire joint structure of the shoulder. Trauma sufficient to break the collarbone can also affect the ligaments and joint structure of the shoulder on the same side.

Shoulder Injuries

Shoulder injuries can be extremely painful and disabling for the victim. The shoulder is the only joint of the body that rotates and articulates 360 degrees. Surgical repairs, such as repair of a rotator cuff tear, typically call for the patient to undergo physical therapy to restore strength and range of motion. Therapy for the shoulder is often quite painful. Patients who avoid full cooperation with therapy often develop a secondary condition called *adhesive capsulitis*, or "frozen-shoulder syndrome." This is a truly painful and disabling condition that requires a subsequent surgery to break loose the adhesions and restore shoulder function. Damage to the shoulder may be isolated to fracture of the bones of the upper arm (humerus), glenoid bone, and the scapula. Any derangement of the bones typically requires surgical repair.

The shoulder or pectoral girdle has no weight-bearing function. The joint structure allows the shoulder to move in more than sixteen hundred positions, providing extensive use and ability for the arms and hands. The downside of the flexibility of this joint is the lack of joint stability and the susceptibility to injury and damage. This ball-and-socket type joint is extremely shallow, with the ball at the upper end of the humerus being 25 percent larger than the socket or glenoid on which it sits. Connective tissue called the *labrum* connects the head of the humerus to the glenoid. Sudden trauma can easily tear the labrum and surgical repair is necessary to repair this essential connective tissue. Muscles and tendons then cover the bony structure to prevent the shoulder from sliding too far in any direction. This structure is known as the "rotator cuff."

The rotator cuff functions just as its name suggests. Four short muscles and tendons form a cuff that wraps around the shoulder joint, allowing the arm to rotate through its full range of motion. If the rotator cuff is torn, the patient will experience pain, limited arm strength, and limited range of shoulder motion.

Rotator cuff tears can vary in severity. A slight, partial-thickness tear is often less problematic and can often be addressed through physical therapy alone. A full-thickness tear will prevent proper function of the shoulder. This is also an extremely painful condition until appropriately restored. The most obvious, common symptom of a full-thickness rotator cuff tear is an inability to reach above shoulder level or to perform any meaningful function with the hand when reaching above shoulder level. Severe pain with movement and severe pain when resting on the injured shoulder are also common symptoms of a torn rotator cuff.

While an automobile accident is a common mechanism of rotator cuff injury, these injuries can also result from sports or from repetitive overhead arm movement. The amount of force required to tear the rotator cuff varies depending on the victim's age, the type of injury, and the extent of degenerative changes in the shoulder joint. Overuse can cause a tear, and a tear can also occur as a result of a dislocation of the upper arm from the glenoid.

Tendonitis of the shoulder is another common cause of shoulder pain. A tendon is a hard fibrous cord that attaches muscle to bone. Tendonitis of the shoulder refers to an inflammation or swelling of the rotator cuff tendons caused by excessive pressure on the acromion (the lump that may be palpated at the top of the shoulder). Tendonitis is typically not caused by sudden trauma. However, there are exceptions and trauma can certainly worsen tendonitis symptoms.

A shoulder dislocation is another common collision-related shoulder injury. The dislocation may be brief and, therefore, not apparent after the bones move back into place. If the shoulder remains dislocated, medical efforts forcing the humerus back into proper anatomical position will alleviate symptoms. Following a dislocation, the shoulder remains vulnerable to reinjury. Ligaments can be torn or stretched during the initial trauma, and the labrum and rotator cuff can also be torn. A full shoulder separation involves the stretching or tearing of the ligaments of the acromioclavicular (AC) joint or the soft tissues that hold the clavicle and scapula together. This condition results from a direct blow to the shoulder or from the patient's effort to brace for collision impact. Drivers often straighten their arms and brace themselves by clenching the steering wheel to prepare for impact. This can cause severe damage to the wrist and to the shoulder. While the arm is held straight, the arm bones are moved suddenly rearward as the patient's body comes forward upon impact. This can separate the shoulder joint significantly. There are six degrees of shoulder separation based on the patient's symptoms.

Early settlements should be avoided in all shoulder injury cases. Insurance carriers often push for early settlements, as they know that shoulder injuries can be persistent. Further, physicians often begin with conservative physical therapy before more expensive diagnostic imaging studies are undertaken. Thus, the true nature and extent of the shoulder injury is often first discovered several months after the accident. Insurance carriers know that an early settlement will allow them to avoid the cost of surgery and their full financial responsibility for medical care costs and pain and suffering.

Hand and Wrist Injuries

Hand and wrist injuries are extremely common in motor vehicle accident cases. The hand is an extremely complicated structure consisting of twenty-seven bones and a variety of soft tissues. Injury to the hand can have a profound impact on the victim's quality of life.

Wrist injuries are properly considered alongside hand injuries and often occur together. The wrist structure consists of the elements of the distal radius and distal ulna (the two bones of the lower arm), the complex of ligaments and fibrous connective tissue, and the carpal bones and other ligaments and bony structures of the hand. Intra-articular wrist fractures, which are fractures through the midline of a joint, are extremely common for those who use their hands to brace for impact. Because of the complex nature of the hand and wrist, these injuries often produce permanent limitations in strength and range of motion. Chronic pain is also a common result. Unfortunately, significant fractures to the hand and wrist carry a high risk for the patient later developing arthritis near the fracture sites.

The carpal bones are the eight bones that separate the metacarpal bones of the hand and the two long bones of the lower arm. These eight bones of the wrist are organized into two rows and form the carpus. Damage to the carpal bones can cause a complex array of difficulties for the patient. Fractured fingers can also be extremely painful and permanent injuries. If surgery is offered as an option, the patient is typically well advised to undergo the procedure. It is best to restore these bones into proper anatomical alignment to ensure proper future function.

Carpal tunnel syndrome is a painful condition that occurs occasionally with trauma. In most cases, carpal tunnel syndrome arises from repetitive motion and is commonly diagnosed as a work-related injury. Typists and factory workers are often susceptible to this condition. Carpal tunnel syndrome occurs because of damage to the median nerve, which passes under the ligament that connects the carpal bones of the wrist. The thumb and first three fingers are involved in the sensory distribution of the median nerve. Carpal tunnel syndrome symptoms typically include pain or numbness to this area of the hand.

Trial verdicts can be very high in hand-injury cases. This is especially true in cases involving crush injury or amputation. Because the hands are involved in almost every day-to-day function, jurors understand the impact of these injuries on the victim's quality of life. The injury claim presentation should include careful research and medical narrative opinions outlining all future limitations imposed by hand and wrist injuries. A functional capacity evaluation or similarly detailed patient evaluation should be conducted to show measurable decreases in grip strength, range of finger and wrist motion, ongoing pain, and all other symptoms. If arthritic changes or other future problems are medically expected because of trauma, a doctor's estimate of all costs for future pain medication and other future medical care should also be provided to support the full value of a hand- or wrist-injury claim. The patient's hobbies and activities should also be considered to show how the hand or wrist injury impacts recreation and quality of life.

Hip Injury

Hip and pelvic injuries are extremely serious and disabling. This large ball-and-socket joint is susceptible to fracture and soft-tissue injury. There is also a true risk of latent injury involved in hip trauma. A brief dislocation can occur. If the bones fall back into place, the patient may not be aware of any damage. Further, X-rays would indicate that the hip is back in proper anatomic alignment. Unfortunately, the damage from a brief dislocation can result in a condition known as *avascular necrosis.*

The hip joint is the area where the head of the femur (the top of the thigh bone) articulates into the pelvis. In a brief dislocation, the head of the femur is torn away from the pelvis. This sudden dislocation can sheer away the blood vessels at the head of the femur, which nourish the bones of the hip and the joint socket. After the femur falls back into place, the hip appears normal and the damage to the blood vessels is not evident. However, over a period of several months, the bones of the hip are malnourished and slowly die. *Necrosis* refers to death of the bone tissue. Football legend Bo Jackson is well known for this injury. After a brief dislocation that was quickly put back in place, he believed that he had recovered from his hip injury. Because of avascular necrosis, he experienced increasing problems several months later and soon had to undergo full hip-replacement surgery.

In cases involving avascular necrosis, hip replacement (arthroplasty) is the only proper repair. Unfortunately, the prosthetic hip is not a permanent installation. The prosthetic joint wears over time, can become unstable, or can become the site of infection. Patients with hip replacements can expect to undergo additional future surgeries to replace the prosthetic hip joint every ten to fifteen years following the initial installation. While many mistakenly assume this is a simple procedure, a hip revision (surgical replacement of a prosthetic hip joint) is actually a far more complicated, invasive, and dangerous surgery than the initial hip replacement. In fact, many doctors who handle hip replacements refuse to handle hip revision and they refer these patients to specialized surgeons with experience in this arena.

Pelvic fractures can be extremely complex and disabling. The pelvis is the core of the skeletal structure and is the fulcrum and balance point for the body. Damage to the pelvis can therefore permanently affect one's ability to walk, balance, or perform basic functions. Because the nerves of the spine terminate at the pelvis, pelvic injuries can also result in loss of bladder and sexual function and other significant sensory deprivation arising from nerve damage.

Patients with severe hip injuries are often transferred from the hospital directly into nursing-care facilities for aggressive rehabilitative therapy. Careful attention should be paid to all medical details in these high-value cases. The patient often has to learn to walk again and is weaned back to weight bearing through a course of painful therapy. Close review of physical therapy notes and all medical records will reveal the difficult road to recovery. After the recovery, the effect on gait, leg length, strain on the back and other areas of the body, and ongoing pain and limited range of motion must be addressed in detail.

Future impact on earning potential should also be considered in all hip-injury cases. A vocational rehabilitation expert can work with physicians and a certified life care planner to nail down all costs of future medical care, all loss of earning capacity, and any apparent future limitations that may require early retirement for the victim.

The most common side effect of hip replacement / arthroplasty is the dislocation of the joint soon after the surgery. The artificial ball and socket are smaller than the one the patient had previously. Thus, the new ball can become displaced with certain movements. Infection, blood clots, and abnormal bone growth are also common side effects of this surgery. As time goes by, tiny particles from the prosthetic may also break off and become absorbed into the surrounding tissue. This process often triggers an inflammatory reaction that causes the implant to loosen.

Do not allow the insurance carrier to minimize the seriousness of a hip fracture. According to the National Center for Injury Prevention and Control, hip fractures cause the greatest number of deaths and lead to the most severe health problems of all injury-related fractures. The victim may become permanently disabled and wheelchair-bound and be confined to a long-term care facility.

Permanent impairment guidelines should also be carefully followed and applied in hip-injury cases. Physicians will consider percentage loss of use of the injured hip/leg and provide a permanent impairment rating for the patient. These impairment ratings can be quite significant. For example, American Medical Association guidelines note that excision of the head and neck of the femur translates to a 50 percent loss of the use of the affected limb. Total hip replacements have an average rating of between 60 and 66 percent loss of use of the leg. For best permanent impairment results, hip fractures should not be evaluated for permanency until two years after initial repair, and current X-rays should be reviewed to rule out aseptic or avascular necrosis or loosening of the hardware.

Because the prosthetic hip is not a permanent fix, many surgeons will perform lesser surgeries with the hope of holding off on complete arthroplasty. The following four additional procedures are commonly seen following traumatic hip injury:

- *Hip Hemiarthroplasty*—This is a less complicated alternative to a full hip replacement. The procedure involves removal and replacement of the head/ball of the femur while leaving the hip socket alone. This procedure accounts for one-third of all hip replacements currently performed. The surgery is less invasive and less expensive and carries a very high success rate. Less than 10 percent of patients will require further surgery.
- *Hip Osteotomy*—This procedure involves cutting away sections of the bone from the femur or the pelvis to alter the shape of the damaged hip joint. The surgeon is essentially seeking to shift the patient's body weight to a joint position with healthier cartilage, thereby reducing the stress on the hip joint. This procedure typically addresses degeneration and is rarely performed in cases involving traumatic hip injury.

- ***Hip Arthrodesis***—This is an invasive procedure that eliminates pain but also eliminates movement and function of the hip joint. The procedure involves fusion of the femur to the pelvis. All hip joint surfaces are surgically removed, and the hip joint is then fused in place with plates and screws. Following the surgery, the patient will still have a meaningful measure of physical function. However, immobility of the hip joint typically results in secondary conditions, such as pain in the back, knees, and the other hip.

- ***Core Decompression***—This procedure is utilized to address avascular necrosis. The surgery involves drilling holes in bones of the hip joint to reduce pressure. It is not always successful. Avascular necrosis causes abnormal pressure to build in the bones of the hip joint, and drilling holes into the necrotic area reduces pressure, which stimulates bone growth and increases blood flow. Drilling holes in the shaft of the femur will create an area of weakness in the bone. Thus, the patient will be susceptible to future hip fracture during the first weeks after the surgery.

Hip injuries produce devastating consequences. Victims of these injuries often endure chronic pain and limited mobility. Statistics confirm that a hip fracture can shorten the victim's life expectancy and result in future complications, such as avascular necrosis and avascular arthritis. These factors must be thoroughly confirmed and explained in the presentation of the hip-injury claim.

Knee Injury

Knee injuries are extremely common in motor vehicle accident cases. In automobile collisions, drivers and passengers will brace for impact by pressing their feet against the floorboard. As the body is propelled forward, this can cause compression trauma and/or a twisting injury to the knee. In frontal impacts, the victims are often thrown forward, causing the knee to impact the dashboard or seat back. In motorcycle, bicycle, and pedestrian collisions, knee trauma produced when striking the pavement can cause severe fracture and soft-tissue damage.

The knee is the most inherently unstable joint of the body. The knee is the union between the femur (the long bone of the thigh) and the tibia and fibula (the two bones of the lower leg). These bones are held together by four primary ligaments:

1. the anterior cruciate ligament (ACL),
2. the posterior cruciate ligament (PCL),
3. the lateral collateral ligament (LCL), and
4. the medial collateral ligament (MCL).

The patella, or kneecap, sits at the front of the knee. This is a cartilage cap that feels and performs like bone and shields the front of the knee joint. The meniscus is a two-part pad that cushions the union between the upper leg bone and the two lower leg bones. The meniscus can be worn thin or torn through years of use or by direct impact and trauma to the knee. Tears to the meniscus can cause significant sharp pains and difficulty when walking, jumping, or climbing/descending stairs.

When describing the instability of the knee, some doctors compare the knee to two matchsticks held together by rubber bands. This description simply explains the inherent instability of the joint. The elasticity of the knee ligaments and the flexibility of the joint create a high susceptibility to injury whenever trauma occurs. Unfortunately, most traumatic injuries to the knee will not heal over time. While physical therapy can be utilized to strengthen the muscles and to increase range of motion and decrease pain, underlying damage to the joint capsule typically will require surgical repair.

Most knee surgeries are performed arthroscopically. Thus, the repair is not terribly invasive and surgical results are typically quite positive for the patient. Knee injuries are commonly overlooked or misdiagnosed. While X-rays will show obvious dislocation of the bones of the knee joint, an MRI is typically the best diagnostic tool to reveal the true extent of ligament, nerve, and soft-tissue damage.

The medical claim presentation in a knee-injury case should include a narrative report from an orthopedic surgeon. The full surgical report will

164

also demonstrate all steps undertaken in surgery. If symptoms persist after surgery, physical therapy and occasionally a second surgical procedure will be required. If the victim had no prior problems with knee pain prior to the collision, it is wise to provide past medical records to confirm that the subject collision was the true cause of the claimed knee injury. The knee injury case presentation should also describe the impact of this injury on the patient's hobbies, day-to-day activities, and lifestyle. Also, proof of permanency, the potential need for and cost of future medical care, and the medical expectation of future symptoms and suffering must be proven to secure proper compensation for a knee injury.

Foot Injury

Traumatic foot injuries can be terribly painful and profoundly disabling. Because all body weight is supported by the feet with every step, foot injuries are slow to heal unless the patient avoids weight bearing entirely. Foot pain can also cause a tremendous amount of minute-by-minute discomfort for the victim.

Certain foot conditions occur by repetitive use and commonly appear without trauma. One example is plantar fasciitis. This condition causes a tremendous amount of pain when walking. While trauma can cause or increase symptoms of plantar fasciitis, the condition is typically degenerative. Podiatrists confirm that pain associated with this condition can prevent almost all physical function for a patient.

The foot is made up of twenty-six bones and more than one hundred muscles, joints, and ligaments that work together to facilitate balance and movement. Because the feet bear all body weight, they are subject to enormous pressure and punishment. During an average day, a person spends about four hours standing and takes up to ten thousand steps. Also, each foot independently bears the full weight of the body and a person's body weight is distributed over just five points when the foot is on the ground. These contact points include the heel and the four end points of the other long bones of the foot.

Improper shoes are a primary cause of foot pain. However, trauma is also a common source of foot problems. Twenty percent of all drivers in car accidents sustain at least one lower-extremity fracture with the foot and ankle sustaining the highest rate of breaks. Statistics show that foot and ankle trauma accounts for 8 to 12 percent of all moderate to severe injuries sustained in frontal collisions. Patients who suffer foot fractures show no improvement six to twelve months after the initial injury, and only 58 percent return to work on a full-time basis after one year.

Anatomically, there are two surfaces of the foot, the dorsal (or top) section and the plantar (or bottom) section of the foot. Doctors identify three major sections of the foot: the forefoot, the midfoot, and the hind foot. Although many bones provide the foundation and flexibility of the foot, the arches of the foot support the weight of the human body. The foot has three arches formed by the metatarsal bones. The highest and most important arch is the medial arch. This is the familiar arch located on the inside middle portion of the foot. Height and elasticity of the arch help to absorb shock and support body weight and balance. The lateral arch is on the outside of the foot and has only slight elevation. This arch is maintained by two strong ligaments. The third arch is the transverse arch, which stretches across the width of the foot. Severe foot fractures can result in a collapse of the bones that form a spring-like frame and guide overall foot function. These injuries are always permanent. Invasive surgery may require installation of screws, plates, and other hardware. Because of the typical extent of use and flexion of the foot, hardware can easily become loosened, which would require later repair or removal. Nerve damage is also quite common and can produce extensive, chronic pain.

Foot drop is another complication arising from foot injury. This is a neuromuscular disorder that affects the victim's ability to raise or move the foot at the ankle inward or outward. The condition is often only a symptom of a larger problem, such as a back problem involving the peroneal nerve deep within the low back. This condition can arise from sciatic nerve trauma, a fractured leg or vertebra, a crush injury, or medical conditions, such as stroke, tumor, or diabetes. Development of foot drop is also a common result of total knee replacement. Considering the various causes of foot drop, detailed medical evidence must show the connection between foot drop and collision trauma.

Foot fractures constitute 10 percent of all broken-bone cases. The foot contains one-quarter of the bones in the body. The soft tissue and ligament structure is extremely complex and highly susceptible to traumatic injury. In all foot-injury cases, care should be taken to consider the obvious and primary diagnosed injuries *and* any potential complications that may arise over the balance of the victim's lifetime. Insurance adjusters will not offer a proper settlement unless detailed medical evidence confirms the true extent of the foot injury and all past and future symptoms.

Careful attention should be invested in the preparation and presentation of all foot-injury cases. Insurance companies always try to argue that foot pain is secondary to age or degeneration. Because physicians have difficulty unraveling the origin of foot pain, they may be reluctant to offer a clear medical opinion relating the foot pain to the motor vehicle collision. Careful research and analysis should overcome these complications. Ultimately, the plaintiff's burden of proof at trial is by preponderance of the evidence. Thus, you need only show that the foot pain and condition were, more likely than not, caused by the vehicle collision. When seeking this medical evidence, the physician's attention should be focused on all pre-accident and post-accident difficulties and all diagnostic imaging and test results before answering whether the claimed foot injury was a result of the accident. Proper medical evidence motivates large settlements and verdicts in foot-injury cases.

CHAPTER 7

❖

LITIGATION AND TRIAL

Insurance carriers always hope to hold back some measure of victim compensation during settlement negotiations. While most cases do settle privately, there are some situations where the insurance carriers and victim cannot agree on case value. In these instances, suit must be filed and the case then moves toward a public jury trial.

The North Carolina Civil Practice Act provides the general rules governing the parties in civil litigation. The North Carolina evidence code is the statutory source governing the admissibility of evidence at trial. These statutes and the case law interpreting them are extremely complex, and a thorough discussion of trial practice and strategy is beyond the scope of this work. However, a general understanding of the litigation process is important as you consider whether to settle your claims privately or to bring your case forward through trial.

In this chapter, we review the primary legal issues relating to injury trial practice. We also explore the steps involved in filing suit, conducting discovery, presenting evidence, and conducting a jury trial.

Parties in the Civil Action

The victim who files a lawsuit is called a *plaintiff*. If two victims suffer injury or loss due to the same accident, they can file a single lawsuit together. The party against whom suit is filed is called a *defendant*. If multiple parties contributed to causing the plaintiff's losses, they are all named in the single action. If a defendant is the sole target of a lawsuit, but he or she believes that outside parties contributed to causing the plaintiff's damages, he or she may file a *third-party action* and thereby bring the outside party into the initial lawsuit as a codefendant.

It is essential to identify and name all parties when filing the initial lawsuit. This is especially true when suit is filed close to the statutory deadline. For example, if a defendant driver causes a serious accident and the defendant was working for a large corporation when the accident happened, the plaintiff can collect from the defendant driver and from the corporation that employed the defendant. However, if the plaintiff files suit close to the three-year deadline and names only the defendant driver, and if the suit filing deadline passes before the employer corporation is named in the action, the plaintiff loses the right to file any action or collect any compensation from the corporation. File your action early, and use the court's discovery tools to identify all necessary parties. This allows ample time to include all parties and all insurance carriers who might be responsible to pay for all injury and accident claims.

Choice of Venue

Venue means the location of the trial. In North Carolina, the victim is allowed to choose the county where the lawsuit will be filed. Pursuant to N.C.G.S. 1-82, the civil action may be filed in the county where the plaintiff resides or where the defendant resides, and if none of the parties reside in North Carolina, the action may be filed in any county that the plaintiff chooses.

Almost all injury cases are filed in North Carolina's state court system. However, in rare cases, attorneys choose to file the action and litigate in federal court. Under 28 U.S.C. 1391, venue in federal civil actions is proper in:

1. a judicial district in which any defendant resides, if all defendants reside in the same state;
2. a judicial district in which a substantial part of the events or errors giving rise to the claim occurred; or
3. if there is no district anywhere in the United States that satisfies 1 or 2, a judicial district in which any defendant is subject to the court's "personal jurisdiction" with respect to such action.

Choice of venue can be very important in North Carolina. Small rural counties tend to be extremely conservative, and juries in these areas render surprisingly low verdicts even in serious injury cases. Major metropolitan areas are typically more favorable for the injury victim. If more than one county is available as a viable trial venue, legal research should be conducted to compare verdict trends in each alternative venue/county. If the counties have relatively similar verdict trends, the plaintiff should choose his or her home county. Since the trial would be conducted in the county where suit is filed, it also wise to consider the location of doctors and other witnesses who may be called to attend trial when selecting the most appropriate trial venue.

Suit Filing Deadlines and Procedure

Deadlines for filing suit are strictly enforced. Failure to file proper pleadings that name and identify *all* liable parties results in a bar and forfeiture of otherwise valid claims. Also, certain exceptions might apply. For example, if the injury victim is a minor child or is mentally incompetent, these conditions may toll or pause the time clock and allow additional time to file. In all cases, the victim should secure an exact deadline from an experienced trial attorney. Through a free consultation, you can learn the exact date of your suit filing deadline and determine whether any time limitations might threaten the loss of your rights of compensation.

Generally speaking, the suit-filing deadline in a nonfatal personal injury case or property damage claim is three years from the date of the collision (N.C.G.S. 1-52). In wrongful death actions arising from fatal accidents, the statutory deadline is two years (N.C.G.S. 1-53).

Simply filing your lawsuit will not suffice to meet the statute of limitations deadline. To properly commence litigation, the plaintiff must identify and name all parties. Failure to include a necessary party at the time of the initial filing forfeits the right to bring later claims against that party after the statutory deadline passes. Further, beyond identifying and naming all proper parties, the plaintiff must also follow all applicable substantive and procedural law in the drafting of the complaint, properly specify all claims presented, and have a proper and enforceable summons issued in conjunction with the civil filing for each party who might be liable for the plaintiff's damages.

The summons is the court document that commands the defendant to enter an appearance before the court and respond to the plaintiff's complaint by filing either a motion or an answer. The summons is a strictly time-limited document and must be served properly on the party defendant named in the summons and complaint pursuant to the strict terms of N.C.R.C.P. 4. The summons can be renewed and extended, and service on the named party must occur before the summons expires. In most cases, service occurs when an agent of the sheriff's office hand-delivers the complaint and summons to the named party. Once suit is filed and all defendants are properly served with the complaint and summons, the injury suit is underway.

District Court Versus Superior Court

In the state court system, the district courts and the superior courts have concurrent, overlapping jurisdiction. District court is the proper venue in smaller cases. The procedure is slightly different, and these cases typically move more quickly through the court system. The jurisdictional limit for civil actions in district court is $25,000.00 or less. This amount was increased from $10,000.00 effective August 1, 2013, pursuant to N.C.G.S. 7A-210 and 7A-243. If the amount claimed in your lawsuit will exceed $25,000.00, the only choice of jurisdiction would be the superior court.

Most injury lawsuits are filed in superior court. The proceedings are more formal, the jurisdictional limit is higher, and the judges are more accustomed to presiding over injury trials. The primary advantage of a district court filing is the potential for collecting attorneys' fees for the plaintiff. N.C.G.S. 6-21.1 allows the district court judge, in the court's discretion, to award the plaintiff their attorneys' fees on top of the injury award. The purpose of the statute is to balance the scales so that plaintiffs with meritorious but small cases are not discouraged from pursuing those claims because they have to pay an attorney.

Small Claims Court

Small claims actions are typically brought by private citizens who have no legal representation. While this is a useful forum for small claims, the party who loses in a magistrate action is entitled to appeal and a *trial de novo*. This is a new trial, which occurs in district court and allows the losing party to eliminate the small claims court victory. Because of the importance of personal injury matters, injury claims typically should not be filed in the North Carolina small claims system. The jurisdictional limit for a small claims action is $10,000.00. If your case might exceed this value, the magistrate's award is strictly limited to the $10,000.00 figure.

Federal Court

In the motor vehicle injury context, litigation in federal court is quite rare. During my years practicing as an insurance defense lawyer, we would often remove an action from state court and pull it into the federal system. This defense tactic essentially took control of the case away from the plaintiff's counsel and pushed the victim into a more formal trial setting. Plaintiffs' lawyers will choose to file suit in federal court only if they expect the likely verdict range to be higher. However, federal judges are typically dealing with significant constitutional cases and claims and matters involving application of the statutes embodied in the United States code. If they perceive the plaintiff as venue shopping and using federal resources unnecessarily, they may be less receptive toward hearing your claims and motions.

As a general rule, the state court system is preferred in personal injury matters. To determine whether your claim may be brought in federal court or removed to federal court by the defendants, see Article 3 of the United States Constitution and 28 U.S.C. 1332.

Defendant's Initial Court Filings

Once defendants are served with the summons and complaint, they are commanded by the terms of the summons to enter an appearance with the court. The summons will call for some response within thirty days. Under the North Carolina Civil Practice Act, a defendant may unilaterally request an additional thirty days to file an answer or other responsive pleading. Defense attorneys always take advantage of this additional time. Therefore, you should expect sixty days to pass after service of your summons and complaint before you receive any responsive court filings from the defense.

The defendant's answer will be a direct response to the individually numbered paragraphs and allegations of the plaintiff's complaint. The answer will also include any other affirmative defenses that might bar or defeat the plaintiff's claims. Careful legal consideration should be given to every word of the defendant's answer and other responsive filings. In some cases, the defendant will file a motion or other responsive pleading that does not include an answer. These responses typically contest the court's jurisdiction over that party or the propriety of the plaintiff's complaint, plaintiff's summons, or plaintiff's effort to deliver the summons and complaint to a proper party in a timely fashion. Careful attention must be given to all responsive pleadings to avoid legal forfeiture of valid claims.

If the defendant is properly served and fails to file an answer, this results in default. Here, all of the allegations contained in the plaintiff's complaint are deemed admitted. If the defendant was properly served and the court indeed has jurisdiction over the party and the subject matter of the plaintiff's claims, the plaintiff in default is allowed to pursue a default judgment. Here, the plaintiff is still required to prove damages before the court will award a dollar judgment.

The Discovery Process

Under the North Carolina Civil Practice Act, the first four-month period after the defendant answers is the *discovery period* of litigation. Attorneys often refer to this as the homework phase of the case. The discovery process allows all parties involved in the lawsuit to assert requests against other parties and force disclosure of information and documents. The four-month discovery period is typically extended by private agreement between the parties and will extend up to the actual trial date.

Because of the rarity of federal litigation in motor vehicle injury cases, I limit my discussion of the discovery rules to only those rules that apply in North Carolina's district and superior courts. For details concerning the scope and rules of discovery in federal trials, see the full text of the Federal Rules of Civil Procedure at www.federalrulesofcivilprocedure.com.

Scope of Discovery

Injury victims are often shocked by the scope of discovery and the extent to which defendants can explore their private and personal affairs. Filing a lawsuit truly does open your life and your medical history to invasive scrutiny. Under N.C.R.C.P. 26(b), a party may discover any matter relevant to the subject matter of a pending action that is not privileged. Privilege refers to legally protected private discussions or information. For example, attorney-client conversations are private and are protected from forced disclosure. The most common privileges protected by North Carolina evidence law are as follows: self-incrimination, doctor-patient, attorney-client, cleric-penitent, husband-wife, and the executive privilege to protect official secrets.

In practice, understand that you may be forced to disclose everything about your medical past, psychiatric treatment and history, criminal past, family history, and other details. Your career and work history can also be explored. You can be compelled to deliver personal income tax filings and other personal financial information. Although much of this information may be excluded from the jury's eyes at trial, all of the information can be demanded by the defense in discovery. Similarly, the plaintiff is also allowed broad latitude to disgorge information from all defendants.

Tools of Discovery

To collect information from opposing parties, the following discovery tools are available to all parties involved in active civil litigation:

- ***Oral Depositions***—Under N.C.R.C.P. 27 and 30, any party may demand the verbal testimony of other parties and witnesses who have information relating to the cause of action. A deposition is simply a question-and-answer session conducted by the party's attorneys. The testimony is provided under oath and subject to legal penalties of perjury. A court reporter will be present to transcribe the verbal testimony for later use as substantive trial evidence or to impeach inconsistent testimony provided by the same witness during the trial.

- ***Written Depositions***—Written depositions are allowed under the North Carolina Civil Practice Act. However, these are very rare and typically ill advised. In some cases, a telephone deposition may be set up, or with recent technology, a video deposition may also be secured by consent or court order. The taking of written depositions is governed by N.C.R.C.P. 31.

- ***Interrogatories to Parties***—The limits and scope of interrogatories are governed by N.C.R.C.P. 33. Interrogatories are written questions that must be answered honestly and under oath by other parties involved in the lawsuit. This is the most common discovery tool. One party may serve any other party with written questions to be answered under oath within thirty days. By agreement, the parties can extend the time to answer. If the party served with interrogatories is a corporation, business, association, or government agency, answers must be provided by any officer or agent designated by that party. If a party objects to questions being asked, the objections must be served on the interrogator along with the reasons for objection. If the deponent refuses to answer an interrogatory or objects to a question, the proponent of the question may file a motion to compel with the court seeking an order compelling an answer. In North Carolina, the requesting party may not serve more than fifty interrogatories, including subparts, unless the court grants leave or the other party agrees.

- ***Request for Production of Documents***—If you seek insurance policies, medical records, or other documentary evidence, this discovery tool accomplishes your objective. A party may serve on any other party a request to produce and permit inspecting and copying, photographing, testing, and sampling of documents, papers, books, objects, or tangible things or demand entry onto land for the purpose of inspecting, surveying, or testing (N.C.R.C.P. 34). These requests may be served on the plaintiff after the commencement of the lawsuit and on any other party after the complaint is served. A party served with such a request must serve a written response within thirty days (forty-five days after service of complaint for the defendant). The response shall either agree to furnish the material or object to the request with specific reasoning. If the response is an objection or refusal to comply, the party submitting the request may move for an order commanding production of the requested documents.

- ***Physical and Mental Examination***—While this discovery tool is rarely used, the defendant can demand that the plaintiff submit to an "independent medical examination" (typically referred to as an IME). Once suit is filed, the victim can be forced to attend a medical examination with a doctor chosen by the defense. Under N.C.R.C.P. 35, when a mental or physical condition of a party is in controversy, the court, for good cause shown, may order that a party submit to a mental or physical examination by a physician chosen and employed by another party. This examination right applies to defendants as well as plaintiffs. While the rule calls for a court order, parties are encouraged to allow an IME by agreement.

- ***Request for Admissions***—This discovery tool allows the parties to refine the facts in dispute and thereby streamline the number of issues to be decided by a jury. Pursuant to N.C.R.C.P. 36, a party may serve any other party with a written request for the admission of the truth of a certain matter, of the application of law to facts, or of the genuineness of documents. Admissions are deemed made unless, within thirty days, the answering party serves a denial, an objection to the propriety of the request (e.g., privileged or irrelevant), or an identification of reasons why he or she cannot admit or deny. An answering party may not give lack of information or knowledge as a reason for failure to admit or deny unless he or she states that he or she has made reasonable inquiry and that the information known or readily obtainable by him or her is insufficient to enable him or her to admit or deny the asserted fact. Aggressive attorneys will use request for admission to nail down the most compelling which confirm legal liability or enhance the value of damage claims.

Benefits of Discovery

A combination of discovery tools can be used to truly understand the defendant's position and the strength of all legal defenses. All discovery responses should be carefully read and considered. The victim's discovery responses should also be scrutinized to unearth the likely arguments the defense will make at trial.

The discovery process sheds light on both sides of the case. Through proper discovery, the plaintiff should demonstrate the strength and value of the plaintiff's injury claims and thereby motivate increases in pretrial settlement offers. Also, thorough discovery and case presentation will increase the likelihood of settlement at the court-ordered mediation.

Mediation—Settlement After Suit Is Filed

In all civil actions filed in superior court, mediation is mandatory and commanded by court order. Mediation is a settlement conference attended by all parties and their attorneys. The mediator is an uninvolved individual who presides over the settlement conference. If the parties cannot agree to a mediator, the court will appoint the mediator who conducts the mediation.

Mediation is truly an opportunity to settle a contested claim. The first portion of the settlement conference is a gathering of all parties and counsel. Here, both sides will present a summary of their claims and defenses to the mediator. Thereafter, all parties will be separated and the mediator will then move from room to room to speak privately with each individual party to the lawsuit. The mediator's goals are to ensure that all voices are fairly heard and considered and to bring the parties to a mutually acceptable settlement if possible. While the mediation is mandatory, settlement is not. The parties are simply commanded to attend the meeting in good faith and make an effort to settle their claims and resolve the lawsuit through private compromise.

As a former claims adjuster and former insurance company lawyer, I encourage accident victims to carefully present their cases at mediation and to be very patient with the process. Use this opportunity to demonstrate the strength of your case. Highlight the trial evidence and show an ability to tell your story with passion. Even if the case is not settled, you should leave a strong impression on the defense. Understand going into the mediation that, while settlement may be achieved, it is often wise to impasse negotiations and leave the mediation without a settlement. This move should not be made on emotion. Rather, if the defense clearly will not extend offers that fall within the likely verdict range, the strength of the plaintiff's position and legal leverage is served by abandoning the negotiations commanded by the court. If the plaintiff's position on legal liability and damages is appropriate and if his or her demand for damages is achievable at trial, the insurance adjusters and insurance defense attorneys who attend mediation will not be able to ignore these factors. If they realize that the plaintiff is not anxious to settle, this may motivate a reevaluation of the case by claims supervisors and defense counsel following the unsuccessful mediation.

The unrealistic victim should also be cautioned. If reasonable offers are extended in mediation and rejected, expect the defense to bear down hard on all evidence, increase their efforts in discovery, and to use the *offer of judgment* to shift their defense costs to the plaintiff. If a fair offer is extended during the mediation, the greedy plaintiff may deeply regret stonewalling and rejecting the settlement opportunity. Through an offer of judgment, the defendant can financially punish a plaintiff who refuses a fair offer and forces an unnecessary trial.

Offer of Judgment

This tool is only available to the defense, and it compels careful consideration by the plaintiff of the offer extended. Through an offer of judgment, a defendant extends a dollar value offer to the plaintiff through the court. These offers have real teeth and should never be ignored. The plaintiff is allowed ten days to accept the stated offer. If the plaintiff fails to respond within ten days or provides an earlier written rejection, this rejection date begins a time clock during which the plaintiff may be held responsible for the defendant's costs incurred defending the lawsuit.

Simply put, the offer of judgment becomes a goal and barrier that must be exceeded by the plaintiff at trial. If the jury verdict does not exceed the offer amount, the defense shall be allowed to collect from the plaintiff, directly or by reduction of the verdict, all costs associated with defending the lawsuit. Typical costs include expert witness fees, court reporter and transcription costs, and expense incurred to preserve evidence and prepare trial exhibits. The defense attorney's legal fees are not included.

Following mediation, defendants will often file an offer of judgment reflecting the last offer rejected at mediation. Thereafter, they can force independent medical examinations, hire medical experts, and extend financial resources to build their defense strategy and evidence. If they are able to hold the plaintiff's verdict down such that it does not exceed the offer of judgment, all of these defense costs will be paid for by the victim. Regretfully, the plaintiff/victim in North Carolina does not have access to this litigation tool or similar legal leverage.

The Jury Trial

The typical docket track in North Carolina is eight to fourteen months. If suit is filed today, this is the amount of time plaintiffs would expect to wait before they actually have their court date and jury trial. As noted above, the early phase of litigation is the discovery phase where the parties are able to investigate all claims and demand disclosure of documents, written answers, and verbal answers from other parties and outside witnesses.

Once the trial date arrives, discovery and case preparation are complete and the case enters the courtroom. The following are the three phases of a typical jury trial in North Carolina

Phase 1: Voir Dire—Jury selection

Voir dire is the legal title of the jury selection process. While the parties may agree to allow the juries to decide all issues through a bench trial without a jury, a jury trial is available in every personal injury case at the request of either party. N.C.R.C.P. 38 and 39 govern the right to a jury trial in a civil case. N.C.G.S. 9-3 governs qualification of jurors and describes those citizens who cannot sit on a jury in North Carolina.

The jury selection process is a question-and-answer session conducted first by the presiding judge and then by the attorneys for each party. The presiding judge makes inquiry to eliminate those jurors who are not qualified to serve. The party's inquiries are made to identify potential jurors who may be biased, interested in the action, or familiar with the litigants. The goal for each side is to identify an unbiased, receptive jury who will decide the case fairly.

Phase 2: Presentation of Evidence and Trial

Once the jury is seated and sworn, the actual trial begins. The jury's sole function is to hear the evidence and determine the facts. In practice, the plaintiff begins the presentation of evidence. Plaintiff's counsel will call witnesses one at a time and, through their testimony and through admission of documentary evidence and other exhibits, provide the jury with evidence that supports the plaintiff's version of the facts. Because the plaintiff has the burden of proof in all injury cases, the accident victim must provide all essential evidence to construct the prima facie case on each required element of every legal claim and on the full amount of all damages sought. If the plaintiff fails to provide necessary evidence, the defense will make a motion at the conclusion of plaintiff's case seeking dismissal of some or all of the plaintiff's claims. After the plaintiff's case is closed, the defense then takes control of the trial and offers evidence to support their version of all contested facts.

The trial begins with opening arguments from both sides. Thereafter, each side takes turns presenting their evidence to the jury. After all evidence is admitted, the parties then present closing arguments. The judge then takes over and reads all instructions to the jury before they retire to decide the case.

Opening and closing arguments are typically the most compelling portion of a trial. The evidentiary phase is typically less dramatic and certainly nothing like what most of us see on television or in movies. The opening argument is limited to a description and forecast provided by each party's counsel of the evidence they expect to present at trial. The closing argument is far more dramatic. Here, parties and attorneys add argument and color to the facts and evidence. In the closing argument, attorneys hope to compel jurors to consider highlighted evidence, to apply evidence to the applicable law, and to reach a verdict in their favor.

Phase 3: Deliberation and Verdict

Jury deliberations are private, privileged, and protected. Once the case goes to the jury, the consideration of the value of the plaintiff's claims lies exclusively with selected jurors. The parties are free to negotiate a settlement during deliberations. However, once a jury reaches a decision on legal liability and case value, their verdict is read in open court and converted to judgment from the bench. The jury's verdict and judgment are the final word on your case. Appeals are only allowed in personal injury cases where significant error is made by the presiding judge in the evidentiary decisions, in the conduct of the proceedings, or in the instructions to jurors.

During deliberations, jurors are not allowed to follow news of the trial, discuss the trial with outsiders, or to speak with parties or attorneys. If they have questions about the evidence or about procedure, procedural rules allow them to bring these to the court's attention and secure answers to facilitate their decision. Once a unanimous verdict is reached, the foreperson who leads the jury will advise the clerk, the judge will recommence the trial proceedings, and the verdict will be read in open court.

Following publication of the verdict, the court will hear motions from both parties concerning the content and effect of judgment. Under North Carolina law, the prevailing plaintiff is entitled to prejudgment interest. The current rate is 8 percent interest, and this amount accrues from the date suit is filed until the date of verdict and judgment. The court will automatically add this amount to the jury's verdict for the benefit of the plaintiff. The prevailing plaintiff may also file a motion asking the court for an award of costs. This is entirely within the judge's discretion. However, in some cases, the defendant is held to pay for the plaintiff's full verdict, and they also are taxed with all of the trial expenses incurred by the plaintiff to conduct the successful trial.

Once the presiding judge signs the order, the plaintiff has a valid and enforceable judgment. At this point, insurance carriers have an actual contractual obligation to pay the plaintiff's judgment in full or to pay the applicable policy limits if the verdict and judgment exceed insurance coverage. If the available insurance is insufficient to pay the trial award, the prevailing plaintiff may then seek to collect the excess judgment by levy against the defendant's personal assets and by filing the judgment to perfect a lien against all real estate owned by the defendant.

Special Proceedings

Before leaving our discussion of the litigation process, certain special proceedings should be understood and considered. Most personal injury cases follow the process outlined throughout this chapter. However, there are unique cases that do not follow the typical pattern of a civil jury trial.

The following special proceedings are undertaken in North Carolina courts;

1. ***Settlement Hearing for Minor/Incompetent***—See chapter 8 for details concerning injuries to a minor child or an individual who is deemed mentally incompetent. Here, we only look to the litigation process involved to perfect a settlement for a minor or a mentally incompetent victim. These settlement hearings are known as a "friendly action." After a settlement is reached, the action is filed simply to bring the case in front of a judge. The plaintiff and the defendant will collectively prepare the complaint and answer. These are filed mutually simply to bring the action onto the court's calendar. The settlement approval hearing is typically heard during a motion calendar. In these hearings, the judge will consider the injuries to the minor or incompetent, the settlement terms, the legal fees and costs, and the propriety of the settlement. This procedure is required to finalize an enforceable settlement in any injury case involving a minor child or a mentally incompetent adult.

2. ***Interpleader Action***—An interpleader is an action filed by an insurance carrier or defendant whereby a certain sum of money is paid into the court so the court can determine the fair distribution of the funds among multiple individuals who have competing claims. The typical scenario is an insurance carrier that has limited coverage and multiple claimants whose claims exceed the available coverage limits. Through an interpleader, the insurer can place the coverage amount with the court and walk away. All claimants are named as defendants in the interpleader action. They are then

required to present their evidence at court to show the full value of their claims. The court's task is then to determine the full value of all parties' claims and then to properly apportion and divide the sum deposited upon filing the interpleader action. The sum is then paid to all claimants based on the court's decision of the fair share to be received by each victim.

3. ***Declaratory Judgment Action***—A declaratory judgment action is a lawsuit filed purely to have the court apply the law to uncontested facts. A common example is an insurance coverage question. If the parties disagree on the effect of insurance policy terms or the application of coverage in a certain case, a declaratory judgment places the legal question before the court to apply contract law and other applicable law to the dispute. Since the parties agree on all material facts, a jury is not required. The facts are stipulated and presented to the judge, and the court determines how the law applies and thus determines the legal rights of all parties.

CHAPTER 8

❖

UNIQUE ACCIDENTS AND SPECIAL CASES

The proceeding chapters provide legal advice and insurance claim guidance that applies in every case. In this chapter, we analyze unique legal situations, unique collision types, and the additional considerations involved in these special cases.

Injury of a Minor Child

North Carolina law provides unique protection to minors. For any child under the age of eighteen, the law deems the minor "incompetent" in the field of contract law. Therefore, a child cannot enter into a binding contract. Because settlement of a personal injury claim is a contractual agreement between the victim and the defense, a child's claim cannot be settled without court involvement. If the value of the child's claim cannot be agreed upon, the child's injury lawsuit proceeds in the same way as an adult victim's case. The only difference would be the involvement of a guardian ad litem, which is a representative included at the court's discretion to confirm that the child's interests have been properly considered by parents, physicians, and plaintiff's counsel.

Settlement for a minor child, to be final and binding, must be reviewed by a trial court judge and approved by court order. In smaller cases (typically claims with a total value of $5,000.00 or less), the insurance carrier may choose to waive the need for court approval. In these cases, they allow the parent/guardian to sign the release and accept the settlement for the benefit of the minor.

If the child's injury claim is settled without court approval, the settlement is not final. Thus, if medical problems arise after the date of settlement, the child's injury claim can be reopened. In fact, the time clock on the three-year statute of limitations in personal injury claims does not start for a minor child until the child reaches age eighteen. Thus, any minor who suffers injury because of another's negligence has until age twenty-one to file suit and commence timely litigation. While the parent's claim for medical expenses is governed and limited by the three-year deadline, the child's claim remains open up to age twenty-one. If the insurance carrier does not insist on court approval, the case can be settled now and later reopened at any point before the victim's twenty-first birthday.

If court approval is involved, this is accomplished through a "*friendly action*". This legal term refers to a consensual lawsuit filed solely to bring the settlement proposal before the court. Judges' approaches to minor settlement hearings differ from county to county and from case to case. Some judges allow informal hearings in chambers, while other judges conduct hearings in open court and carefully consider all case facts and settlement terms. In all cases, the court considers the detailed description of the child's injury and medical treatment, permanency of injury, and the potential need for future care, the total amount of the proposed settlement, the propriety of disbursals for unpaid medical expenses and legal fees, and the plan for disbursal of the child's net settlement proceeds.

When court approval is involved, the child's funds will not be disbursed until the child reaches age eighteen. In rare cases, a motion can be filed with the court to encroach on the settlement fund. Most judges will not allow parental access to the child's settlement money to fund scholastic needs or other obligations that are typically a parent's responsibility. Thus, the family should plan for the child's settlement money to remain invested until the child reaches age eighteen.

There are two options for disbursal once the victim reaches age eighteen. First, most cases involving child injury and court approval leave the minor's proceeds on deposit in an account held and managed by the clerk of court. There is a small administrative fee involved with initial deposit and account maintenance. These accounts do earn interest, which accumulates until withdrawal. At age eighteen, the child claimant can present proper identification and secure a lump-sum withdrawal from the clerk of court. Second, some parents prefer to utilize a structured settlement for the benefit of their injured child.

Structured Settlements

Under current tax law, the proceeds of a personal injury claim settlement are nontaxable. A structured settlement is designed to allow an accident victim to maximize the benefit of this tax law. Structured settlements are commonly used to plan disbursal of a child's settlement to ensure that the funds are paid at preplanned intervals to avoid the risk of an eighteen-year-old beneficiary irresponsibly squandering his or her injury claim proceeds. However, adult accident victims may also choose to structure their settlement so that their accident claims are paid through a series of preplanned installments.

A structured settlement agreement is a private agreement and contract that can be engineered to meet the victim's wishes. For example, in child injury cases, parents often choose to follow a "college-years payout." Instead of the child receiving all of the money at age eighteen, he or she would receive five equal installments beginning on the eighteenth birthday and continuing annually over a five-year period. The court must approve the structured payment plan if the victim is a minor child. If the victim is an adult, he or she is free to create any payment plan that the parties agree to.

A word of caution is warranted concerning structured settlements. There are a number of financial service organizations that advertise payment advances on structured settlements. The structured settlement is an annuity contract whereby the insurance carrier pays money to the victim over time. Because the victim never receives settlement proceeds until the contractual date of disbursal, there is no income tax on these future settlement payments. The annuity contract is an ironclad agreement. They are typically not tied to stock markets or investments, and the future payment is a certainty. The companies that offer advances and early payment typically buy the victim's annuity rights at a *severe* discount. You truly give up a great amount of money to secure these early payments. Thus, plan ahead when considering a structured settlement and make sure that you will not need early access to your settlement proceeds. If you might need access to settlement money sooner, avoid the structure option and take your full settlement as a single lump sum.

Uninsured Driver Accidents

Under the North Carolina Financial Responsibility Act, uninsured motorist (UM) coverage is mandatory and included on all auto policies. If you are struck by a driver who failed to pay insurance premiums to maintain coverage, your claims against the uninsured driver would be covered under your own policy. Under our pure contributory negligence law, you must be entirely innocent of contributory conduct or driver error before you could present any claims against the other driver. This is true regardless of whether the other driver is insured.

If the other driver was not insured, your insurance carrier will defend that driver! In fact, if the claims cannot be settled and a lawsuit must be filed, your insurance company will hire and pay for the lawyer who stands with the uninsured driver in court. The lawyer they pay will argue against you in court and suggest to the jury that you caused your own injuries, that the injury claims are false or exaggerated, and that your injury claims are inflated and unfair. Whenever possible, the lawyer your insurance company hires will try to convince a jury to leave you with a zero verdict following trial.

Immediately after you report a UM claim to your insurance company, they will look closely at the accident facts and seek to blame you for the accident. If you were slightly at fault, they will deny all UM claims. If they do accept legal liability and agree that the uninsured driver caused your accident, they will still challenge the validity and value of all injury claims. It is vital to understand that the UM adjuster's goal is to minimize your injury claim payments. You should not trust them to simply volunteer fair payment for your accident claims. Even though you are presenting claims through your own policy, the UM context places you in direct conflict with your insurance carrier.

Two important points should be considered by the UM claimant. First, pushing your insurance carrier for proper and maximum payment would not cause *any* increase in your auto insurance premiums. They cannot drop your coverage or raise your rates. Thus, you should not be dissuaded from enforcing your rights to fair compensation. Second, in an injury claim against your uninsured motorist coverage, the adjusters represent the at-fault driver exclusively. They will contest all your injury claims, and they will diplomatically pull you toward a discounted settlement. Be prepared to stand your ground.

If the at-fault driver failed to carry insurance, he or she will regret this in the long run. Your insurance carrier retains the legal right to sue that driver and recoup whatever they pay under your UM coverage. As soon as the UM claims are paid and settled, your insurance company will "subrogate" against the uninsured driver. Subrogation means to stand in the shoes of another, and here it means that the UM carrier holds your rights against the uninsured driver. Thus, the law allows them to collect what they pay from the driver who caused your accident. They will first contact that driver and seek a private payment agreement, and if the uninsured driver refuses, your insurance carrier can suspend the uninsured driver's license privilege. If this is not enough to bring the uninsured driver to the table, your insurance company will pay a lawyer to sue the uninsured driver and secure an enforceable judgment. Their goal is to recoup everything they pay out from the driver who violated our mandatory insurance laws.

Your UM insurance carrier protects you after the accident, but they then protect themselves by pursuing the driver who failed to carry liability insurance. Since they have strong legal rights, you should not feel sorry for your insurance company when they are pushed to pay full value for all accident claims. Protect yourself and insist on full and fair payment of all accident claims. If the UM carrier fails to offer a proper settlement, you should continue to fight until you are properly paid.

Most UM claims settle. However, if the adjuster fails to offer a fair settlement, you should continue through the trial process. Fortunately, North Carolina UM law provides an option to the victim who cannot reach a settlement with the adjuster. If the UM claimant does not receive an acceptable settlement offer, he or she can choose a typical jury trial or can instead elect to have the case decided through private arbitration.

Arbitration is a simple proceeding conducted by a three-judge panel. It is a private trial with binding results. The victim and the insurance carrier each pick their own preferred arbitrator. The third arbitrator must be picked by mutual agreement of the parties' preferred arbitrators. The insurer and the victim split the total cost of the arbitration. With all three judges' charges, an arbitration typically costs $1,500.00 to $3,000.00, which, while expensive, is far less than the costs involved in a typical jury trial. Again, these costs are split between the victim and the UM insurance carrier. The rules of trial evidence apply, and the arbitration is essentially a mini-trial where the evidence is presented to the arbitration panel in a private setting. The arbitrators then determine the value of the case, and their case resolution and damage award is binding on the parties.

Uninsured motorist coverage is stackable in North Carolina. Please see chapter 1 for a more detailed discussion of stacking rights and the procedure involved to properly collect benefits from multiple UM policies. Simply put, the victim of an uninsured driver can use several policies concurrently and collect from these multiple sources. Settlement must be made with all applicable policies and insurance carriers simultaneously. If you settle with one policy without sweeping in another outside source, the first settlement closes all claims and forfeits your rights under outside policies. The victim of an uninsured driver can collect from *all* of the following policies:

- the auto policy on the vehicle involved in the collision;
- all outside personal auto policies held by the victim and showing the victim as a named insured; and
- *any* other motor vehicle insurance policy held by any person related by blood or marriage to the victim who resided with the victim on the collision date.

Please remember that insurance carriers always seek to minimize their own financial exposure. In significant injury cases, competent counsel is recommended to ensure that the UM carrier respects the threat of litigation, understands all essential medical evidence, finds and applies all available UM policies, and pays full value for all medical expenses, lost wages, pain, suffering, scarring, disfigurement, and lost quality of life.

Underinsured Motorist Claims

Underinsured motorist (UIM) cases are similar to UM claims. Stacking rules are the same, and thus victims can collect benefits under multiple policies by looking first to the vehicle they were riding in and then to all personal auto insurance policies and all policies for all family members who resided with them on the date of loss.

UIM is different from UM in that the at-fault vehicle and/or driver will have some measure of liability insurance to cover the victim's damages. Although the at-fault party is insured, he or she would be "underinsured" if the total limits of all available liability policies is less that the total limits of all available and stackable UIM policies.

See chapter 1 for an explanation of how UIM coverage is stacked and utilized. In all UIM cases, the victim should be very careful to search for and identify all liability policies. If an excess liability policy is not identified, the UIM carriers will discover the additional liability coverage and then legally reduce or eliminate available UIM benefits. Also, it is imperative to locate all UIM policies before settlement. Failure to identify a UIM carrier may reduce the total coverage and payments available to the victim.

Similar to UM cases, a UIM claim can be arbitrated if the victim and all insurers cannot agree to a private settlement. One very unique aspect to a UIM claim is the ability to split the claim into a two-stage settlement. If liability coverage limits have been offered and "tendered" (meaning that the money is made available to the victim), the victim now has the right to open and present a claim for UIM benefits. Under North Carolina law, adjusters for all stackable UIM insurance policies must be notified of the liability tender offer. Once they receive notice of the liability coverage limit offer, they have thirty days from that point to determine whether they intend to subrogate against the at-fault driver and all other parties who caused injury to the UIM insured.

Through a subrogation claim, the UIM insurance carrier stands in the shoes of the insured victim and they have a right to pursue reimbursement of their UIM claims payments by bringing claims against the parties who caused the auto accident. The UIM insurance carrier can file suit, bring the auto accident case through a trial, and secure a verdict and legal judgment against all parties who caused the injury that is the subject of the UIM claim. For example, if an at-fault driver carries just $30,000.00 in bodily injury liability coverage and this amount is offered to the victim, and if the victim has serious injury claims and UIM coverage of $100,000.00 available under his or her own policy, the UIM carrier faces up to $70,000.00 in financial exposure (the at-fault driver was underinsured by $70,000.00, which is the difference between the total UIM coverage available and the total liability coverage available for that collision). If the UIM insurer pays the full $70,000.00 to the insured victim, they have the legal right to sue the at-fault driver and collect the $70,000.00 that they paid.

Our laws allow the victim to split their claim into two parts and reach the liability limits early. This effectively eliminates the UIM carrier's ability to hold up the liability settlement and coerce the victim/insured to accept a lesser UIM settlement just so they can collect the first layer of payment benefits from the liability policy. In practice, the victim notifies the UIM carrier of the liability limits offer. During the next thirty days, the UIM carrier will perform an asset search to see if the at-fault driver owns real estate or has other wealth worth pursuing. If the at-fault driver has no apparent wealth, the UIM carrier will waive subrogation by allowing the thirty-day time clock to pass without taking any action. If the UIM carrier intends to preserve their right to seek reimbursement from any at-fault party, they must pay the total amount offered by the liability insurance to the insured victim. This payment is called a *UIM advance payment*. The UIM advance payment provides the early payment of liability coverage limits to the victim while, at the same time, precluding the victim from signing any documents or reaching any agreement with the liability insurance carrier.

In most cases, the UIM insurer will choose not to pursue reimbursement from the at-fault parties and they will waive their subrogation rights. Once this occurs, the victim can collect the liability coverage limits directly from the liability insurance carrier. However, to collect the liability benefits early, the victim must forfeit the right to pursue the personal wealth and assets of the at-fault driver. Thus, the victim should perform his or her own asset search to identify wealth and assets for all at-fault parties, and the victim must also identify all UIM policies to calculate the total amount of UIM benefits available. If the total of all UIM benefits would not fully compensate the victim and if the at-fault parties own real estate, stocks, bonds, or other assets, it would be a mistake to settle the liability claim early with the liability carrier. They will only agree to the early payment if the victim signs a *covenant not to enforce judgment*. Thus, they only pay the liability limits if the victim agrees that he or she can never pursue the at-fault driver for payment of any verdict or judgment that exceeds all available UIM policies. Fortunately, if the at-fault parties do have meaningful wealth worth pursuing, the UIM carrier likely would pay the UIM advance payment thereby allowing the victim to enjoy the benefit of the early payment and the two-stage settlement allowed under North Carolina law.

The laws relating to stacking of UIM and the split settlement with liability and UIM coverage are quite complex. If you are dealing with a serious injury case involving an offer of full liability coverage limits, it is wise to secure a consultation with an insurance coverage lawyer to make sure that all of your financial options are clearly understood. Even if you must pay for the legal consultation, you will have peace of mind knowing that all layers of available insurance funding are carefully preserved for your benefit. Insurance carriers are only concerned with closing their claim file, and they will not help you to protect your rights or preserve the ability to collect additional coverage that is outside of their policy.

Hit-and-Run Accidents

We must distinguish between the hit-and-run accident where the driver is later identified and the pure hit-and-run situation. Under North Carolina law, it is illegal to leave the scene of a motor vehicle collision. Thus, the hit-and-run driver commits separate criminal violations when he or she flees the scene. If the driver is later located, his or her conduct of departure is an aggravating factor, which would lead most juries to render a more generous verdict. If there is any allegation that the victim committed a driver error that contributed to causing the accident, the fact of hit-and-run would typically destroy the defendant's credibility and ensure the victim's victory at trial.

If the hit-and-run driver is never located, the victims must present their claims against their uninsured motorist coverage. All of the legal and practical considerations discussed above would apply here. If settlement cannot be reached and the victim prefers trial over arbitration, the lawsuit is filed against "John Doe" and the action proceeds accordingly through a jury trial. In these trials, your uninsured motorist insurance carrier would hire and pay for the lawyer who opposes your claims in court.

Phantom Vehicle Accidents

A phantom vehicle case is similar to a hit-and-run accident. Here, the responsible driver leaves the scene of the accident, and although his or her driving error caused the collision, there was no contact between the responsible driver's vehicle and other vehicles involved. For example, if a truck merges into your lane and you are able to swerve and avoid contact with the truck, any accident that occurs due to your evasive maneuver would be the truck driver's fault. If the truck driver leaves the scene and is never identified, this would be a phantom vehicle case.

Unfortunately, victims of phantom vehicle drivers have few legal rights under North Carolina insurance law. In a typical hit-and-run case, victims can present all claims against the hit-and-run driver under their uninsured motorist coverage. However, the UM policy specifically requires "contact" with the hit-and-run vehicle before coverage would apply. Thus, the victim of the phantom vehicle cannot collect UM benefits. The only claims that are covered by the victim's personal auto policy would be a collision claim for repair or replacement of the vehicle and a medical payments claim to fund medical care costs for all occupants of the insured vehicle. It is truly unfortunate that a victim of a phantom vehicle accident cannot collect for lost wages, pain and suffering, and other obvious losses.

Motorcycle Accidents

The four collision types we discuss next are highly targeted by insurance carriers for defense and claims denial. These are motorcycle accidents, moped/scooter accidents, bicycle accidents, and pedestrian accidents. A common thread among these cases is the severe and occasionally catastrophic injuries that follow from these incidents. Pedestrians and motorcycle riders have very little protection when a collision occurs. Thus, injuries can be devastating, and the victims' claims for medical care costs and lost quality of life can easily exceed all available insurance coverage.

Legal representation in motorcycle accident cases is strongly encouraged. I am a fellow rider, and I understand the unique handling characteristics of motorcycles. You should look for a lawyer who understands how a motorcycle operates and handles and who has dealt with the physics involved in analyzing and reconstructing these unique accidents. Insurance companies target motorcycle accident cases for total denial by using North Carolina's pure contributory negligence law. If the motorcycle rider is *slightly* at fault for causing his or her own accident in North Carolina, he or she has no claims and no payment rights. Even in clear liability cases, adjusters often argue that the motorcycle rider placed him- or herself in a position of danger simply by riding the motorcycle. While the law does not support this position, if a jury misunderstood the law and placed slight blame with the rider, the victim would receive zero compensation for his or her accident claims.

Insurance adjusters also work very quickly to secure written or recorded statements in these cases. They try to trap the motorcyclist into admitting to speeding or failing to take the earliest available evasive maneuver. Also, because the stopping distances, turning capabilities, and handling characteristics of motorcycles are quite different from a car's handling and braking capabilities, they use complex accident reconstruction knowledge to build upon facts that support laying blame with the biker. In fact, they know that many people are afraid to ride motorcycles and they will try to encourage a jury to conclude that the biker "assumed the risk" of injury and thus caused his or her own injuries. This is not a correct application of North Carolina's assumption of risk law. However, if the defense attorney sways the jury in this direction, you could lose the motorcycle injury trial.

When seeking legal counsel in a motorcycle accident case, discuss your case directly with the attorney who will personally handle the case. Look for at least some riding experience. The attorney in a motorcycle accident case should understand the hand-brake, foot-brake, clutch, gear function, and handling traits so he or she can truly understand the details of what you went through before, during, and after impact. Make sure the attorney is prepared to investigate the collision and analyze all collision facts to nail down fault and legal responsibility. While interviewing attorneys, also make sure they have significant experience with serious and catastrophic injury cases. Injuries in these cases are often permanent. However, without admissible medical evidence confirming permanency and the anticipated cost of future medical care, the insurance carrier will not pay for future medical needs or for future pain and suffering.

Careful focus should be applied to the reconstruction of the accident, application of all traffic laws, anticipation of available liability defenses, photography and documentation of *all* physical and emotional injuries, presentation of medical opinion evidence on scarring / permanency / future medical needs, and thorough analysis of jury verdict trends in similar cases. A careful search for additional at-fault parties and additional insurance coverage should be undertaken to access all available funding. Motorcycle accident claims often bring large settlements and verdicts. Thus, thorough medical evidence and all other value factors should be pushed aggressively to secure maximum compensation for the injured rider and his or her family.

Moped / Motor Scooter Accidents

All cautionary advice regarding motorcycle accidents applies to these cases. Additional issues arise when considering the special characteristics of mopeds and scooters. Under current North Carolina law, insurance and a driver's license are not required to operate a motorized scooter or moped with an engine size smaller than 50cc. Maximum speed on these scooters is typically around thirty-five to forty miles per hour. Also, these vehicles can be more difficult to see. *Expect* the insurance company to argue that the scooter rider was partially at fault.

Scooter riders do have the same privilege to share the road as other drivers and bicyclists. However, if they are not reaching the minimum posted speed (for example, driving the scooter on a major highway), this would constitute contributory negligence barring the victim's right of compensation. Another practical truth is many scooter riders choose this mode of transportation because they have lost their driver's license privileges. Insurance carriers will investigate the status of the rider's driver's license and utilize any prior DWI convictions or other criminal history to their advantage.

Bicycle Accidents

With the passage of the comprehensive Bicycle and Bikeway Act of 1974, North Carolina established the first state bicycle program in the nation. Our state's law quickly became a national model. The legislation granted authority for the North Carolina Bicycle Program (now the Division of Bicycle and Pedestrian Transportation) to undertake comprehensive bicycle planning and programming. Obviously, bicycling is very popular in our state.

Bicycle accidents have become quite common, especially in college towns and major metropolitan areas. Inner city dwellers often choose bicycles to avoid traffic and to save fuel. Unfortunately, drivers in these busy areas often fail to watch for bicycles. The resulting accidents can truly be catastrophic.

Rider visibility is a primary focus in bicycle investigations. Insurance adjusters always look at the lighting, reflectors, and the rider's clothing and helmet to determine whether the bicyclist followed all safety rules before attempting to share the roadway. Again, the pure contributory negligence law in North Carolina allows the insurance company to deny all claims if they can show that the bicyclist was just 1 percent at fault. Because a headlight is required by statute, insurance carriers will commonly deny nighttime bicycle accidents if the rider did not have a proper headlight illuminated at the time of impact. Similarly, they look at the rider's clothing and all other actions of the bicyclist purely with an eye toward defending the case and denying liability for all accident claims.

Under North Carolina law, a bicycle has the legal status of a vehicle. This means that bicyclists have full rights to share the roadway, and they are also subject to the traffic laws and regulations governing the operation of a motor vehicle. North Carolina traffic laws require bicyclists to:

- ride on the right side of the road in the same direction as other traffic
- obey all traffic signs and signals
- use hand signals to communicate intended turns and movement
- equip their bicycle with a front lamp visible from three hundred feet and a rear reflector that is visible from a distance of two hundred feet when riding at night
- wear a bicycle helmet on public roads, public paths, and public rights-of-way if the rider is under sixteen years of age

- secure child passengers in a child seat or bicycle trailer if under forty pounds or forty inches in height

Bicyclists are encouraged to be thorough when they present property damage claims. If the bicyclist was innocent, the responsible driver and insurance carrier owe the lesser of repair or replacement of the bicycle. Bicycle design technology is rapidly advancing. Carbon fiber frames and other lightweight components can be very costly. The bicyclist is entitled to the lesser of repair or replacement of the bicycle. There is a strong secondary market for high-end bicycle components. By carefully proving the full value of the bicycle and all safety equipment, you will motivate much higher payments for bicycle damage claims.

Injuries from bicycle accidents can be quite severe. Photographs of all road rash and visible injuries should be taken immediately after the accident. Photograph and video should also be taken during the recovery process, especially when surgery or other aggressive care is involved.

Bicyclists are encouraged to stand strong on their injury claims. Jurors favor bicyclists and appreciate the seriousness of these claims. The only negative bias we see is the occasional case where the bicyclist is involved in an accident on a high-volume roadway when he or she causes congested traffic. In the inner-city accident case, jurors typically sympathize with the injured bicyclist and they render very generous verdicts.

Pedestrian Accidents

Pedestrian accidents are the final accident type targeted by insurance carriers for aggressive defense. Common sense tells us that it is typically easy to avoid being in the roadway or being struck by a vehicle. If the driver leaves the roadway, establishing legal liability is simple. However, if a pedestrian is crossing the roadway away from a marked crosswalk or if he or she is walking on the roadway with his or her back to traffic (violating statutory law), the insurance carrier will typically argue that the pedestrian was at least 1 percent at fault. Beyond the contributory negligence defense, they often also argue that the pedestrian "assumed the risk" of injury by placing him- or herself on or near the roadway. Remember that these are complete defenses in North Carolina and would result in a zero verdict following trial. Do not allow insurance adjusters to blame you if the driver was at fault.

Careful analysis of all North Carolina pedestrian safety statutes should be made in every case. Of key importance are the following laws:

- **N.C.G.S. 20-172**—Pedestrians subject to traffic-control signs and signals
- **N.C.G.S. 20-173**—Rules concerning pedestrians' right-of-way at crosswalk
- **N.C.G.S. 20-174**—Rules for crossing other than crosswalks and walking along roads and highways
- **N.C.G.S. 20-174.1**—Standing, sitting, or lying upon highways or streets prohibited
- **N.C.G.S. 20-175**—Pedestrians soliciting rides, employment, business, or funds upon highways or streets

These statutes and all statutes governing the driver and surrounding traffic should be considered in a pedestrian/auto collision. Also, practical analysis of the lighting conditions, color and shade of the pedestrian's clothing, speed of the vehicle, braking effort of the driver, presence of all traffic controls and signs in the area, and all other facts surrounding the accident must be carefully considered in every case.

If the insurance carrier seeks to blame you for the pedestrian accident, you should consider application of the "last clear chance" doctrine. This doctrine stands as an exception to the contributory negligence defense and allows a negligent pedestrian to collect from the driver's insurance carriers. The last clear chance doctrine has four elements:

1. that the pedestrian carelessly placed him- or herself in a position of peril;
2. that the driver noticed the pedestrian in his or her position of peril, or, through the exercise of reasonable care, could have observed and noticed the pedestrian;

3. that the driver, at the point where he or she should have noticed the pedestrian, had means and opportunity (or a last clear chance) to avoid the pedestrian; and
4. that the driver's failure to avoid the pedestrian caused harm.

Injuries in these cases are often severe, and thus the fourth element is almost always present. Through careful investigation, reconstruction of the accident, and aggressive advocacy, a pedestrian who committed a slight error often can overcome the contributory negligence defense and still collect full payment for injury claims. However, it is essential to prove with certainty that the driver should have seen and avoided you.

Darting child cases are examples of pedestrian cases where the last clear chance doctrine would not apply. An example would be a case where a driver is proceeding at a safe speed when a child suddenly runs between two parked cars directly into the driver's path. If the driver has no prior opportunity to notice the child and if the driver was maintaining a safe lookout and proper speed, this would be a case where the driver would not have a last clear chance to avoid the accident. In these cases, there would be no right to compensation for the injured pedestrian.

Eighteen-Wheeler—Tractor Trailer Accidents

Trucking accidents involve complex legal issues and application of state and federal law. Most long-haul truck drivers carry commercial driver's licenses (CDLs) requiring extensive additional training and testing. Once the CDL is issued, the commercial driver is governed by laws that are significantly stricter, even when they are driving their personal automobile. For example, private drivers can be convicted of driving while impaired if they are found to have a BAC of .08 percent. Holders of a CDL would be convicted of DWI in their private vehicle with a BAC of .04 percent and a DWI in the commercial vehicle with a BAC of .01 percent.

Tractor-trailer drivers are governed by state traffic laws and by the federal motor carrier safety regulations (FMCSRs). The most common North Carolina traffic laws that govern truck drivers are as follows:

- **N.C.G.S. 20-138—Impaired Driving In A Commercial Vehicle**: For commercial drivers, the legal limit for blood alcohol concentration is .04 percent in private vehicles and .01 percent when driving a commercial truck. Federal regulations often require the driver to report voluntarily for BAC testing following an accident. If a sober driver fails to secure this testing, this failure can be admitted as evidence that impairment could have indeed been a factor leading to the collision.

- **N.C.G.S. 20-140—Reckless Driving**: This statute forbids driving "without due caution and circumspection and at a speed or in a manner so as to endanger or be likely to endanger any person or property."

- **N.C.G.S. 20-140.2—Overloaded Vehicle**: Trucks are difficult to handle when cargo is unevenly loaded or overloaded. If cargo was insecure, out of balance, or overweight, this is a violation of our traffic law.

- **N.C.G.S. 20-141—Speed Restrictions**: Speed is often a factor in truck accidents. This statute requires the truck driver to obey all posted limits and prohibits the driver from driving at a speed that is greater than "reasonable and prudent under the conditions then existing." Thus, in rain or heavy traffic, speeding violations can occur even if the driver is traveling within the posted limit.

- **N.C.G.S. 20-146—Drive on Right Side of Roadway**: This statute requires the truck driver to maintain his or her proper lane of travel, to avoid improper lane mergers, and to remain on the right side of any divided road/highway.

- **N.C.G.S. 20-148—Meeting of Vehicles**: This statute requires vehicles approaching in opposite directions to avoid crossing center.

- **N.C.G.S. 20-149—Overtaking a Vehicle**: This statute requires a vehicle that is passing another to leave two feet of space while passing and to return to the right side/lane only when there is sufficient room to do so. This statute also requires the vehicle being passed to yield to the passing vehicle and to maintain speed to allow the pass to occur.

- **N.C.G.S. 20-150—Limitation on Privilege of Overtaking/Passing**: The passing vehicle can initiate a pass only if the oncoming lane is clear, only when the curve or grade of the road allows visibility five hundred feet ahead, and never at double-yellow centerlines or railway crossings.

- **N.C.G.S. 20-151—Driver to Give Way to Overtaking Vehicle**: If a driver is being passed, he or she must not speed up or act in a way to prevent being overtaken.

- **N.C.G.S. 20-152—Following Too Closely**: This is the most common cause of rear-end collisions. Trucks require greater stopping distances than private passenger autos, and truck drivers should be fully aware of the distance required to stop. When a vehicle is struck from behind, this law is the basis for all claims against the truck driver.

- **N.C.G.S. 20-153—Turning at Intersections**: This statute requires drivers turning right to remain as close to the right curb as possible and drivers turning left to yield to oncoming traffic and ensure that the turn can be made without interfering with the safe flow of traffic.

- **N.C.G.S. 20-154—Signals on Starting, Stopping or Turning—** This statute requires a vehicle intending to turn to use visible turn signals and to maintain the visible signal for two hundred feet prior to the intended maneuver whenever the speed limit is forty-five miles per hour or greater. Vehicles that stop must have proper brake lights and signals as well.

- **N.C.G.S. 20-155—Right of Way**: Drivers turning left must yield and give the right of way to oncoming vehicles and to pedestrians in crosswalks. Drivers entering from a driveway, parking area, alley, or side street must yield before entering the adjacent roadway. If two vehicles approach an intersection from different roads at the same time, the driver to the left must yield to the driver to the right.

- **N.C.G.S. 20-158—Vehicle Control Signs or Signals**: If the truck driver disobeyed any signs, painted lines, or traffic controls during the approach to the accident site, this statute provides the basis for legal liability.

- **N.C.G.S. 20-161—Stopping on Highway Prohibited**: This statute, coupled with similar federal regulations, prohibits stopping on the roadway and requires disabled vehicles to be moved (when possible) or clearly identified with warning flares, reflective triangles, etc.

Beyond these state traffic laws, the following Federal Motor Carrier Safety Regulations are commonly encountered in truck accident cases:

- **F.M.C.S.R. 392.3—Ill or Fatigued Operator**: This regulation prohibits the truck driver and the trucking company from continuing a trip when the driver's ability or alertness is impaired or likely to become impaired because of illness, fatigue, or any other cause. There are strict rules governing the number of consecutive hours that a truck driver can legally remain on the road. Truck drivers are also required to maintain driver trip logs and all trip receipts (for meals, fuel, hotel, etc.) to prove that they took required breaks and did not remain on the road any longer than federal laws allow.

- **F.M.C.S.R. 392.4—Drugs or Other Substances**: No driver shall be on duty and possess, be under the influence of, or use any amphetamine, any narcotic drug or derivative thereof, or any other impairing substance.

- **F.M.C.S.R. 392.5—Alcohol Prohibition**: Under federal regulations, a truck driver cannot use alcohol within four hours before going on duty or use alcohol or have any measured alcohol concentration or detected presence of alcohol while operating or in physical control of a commercial vehicle.

- **F.M.C.S.R. 392.6—Schedules to Conform with Speed Limits**: If the trucker was speeding, this regulation allows suit directly against the trucking company if the delivery and trip schedules impose deadlines that cannot be achieved without speeding.

- **F.M.C.S.R. 392.7—Equipment Inspection and Use**: This regulation requires the trucking company and the truck driver to inspect and ensure proper function of the service brakes, trailer brake connections, parking / hand brake, steering mechanism, lighting devices and reflectors, tires, horn, windshield wipers, rear-vision mirrors, and coupling devices.

- **F.M.C.S.R. 392.9—Inspection of Cargo and Cargo Securement Devices**: The truck driver and those involved in loading the cargo are governed by strict regulations that require careful strapping, stacking, balancing, and securing of all cargo before the journey begins. During the journey, the driver is also charged with the legal obligation to check and secure cargo.
- **F.M.C.S.R. 392.14—Hazardous Driving Conditions**: A truck driver is required to use "extreme caution" in hazardous conditions, such as snow, ice, sleet, fog, mist rain, dust, or smoke. If conditions are sufficiently dangerous, the truck driver is legally obligated to immediately discontinue travel and get off the road.
- **F.M.C.S.R. 392.22—Emergency Signals, Stopped Vehicles**: A truck driver is required to follow specific steps to alert approaching traffic whenever his or her truck is stopped upon the traveled portion of a highway or on the shoulder.
- **Miscellaneous Regulations**: The federal regulations impose strict guidelines for drivers (e.g., license requirements, training, log keeping, reporting) and for trucking companies (e.g., hiring requirements, driver record requirements, testing requirements, truck maintenance requirements, etc.).

Truck accident victims should research all applicable laws and identify each and every legal violation committed by the commercial driver and also any violations committed by the trucking company. Cumulative violations may support a claim for punitive damages. Also, if the trucking company pushes the driver to violate laws to meet cargo delivery deadlines, these facts significantly increase the settlement value or verdict range of the victim's claims.

Current federal law requires a truck driver and motor carrier to carry at least $750,000.00 in liability insurance. This is a "per occurrence" limit, meaning that the coverage limit is the full amount available to pay for all property damage and injury claims for all victims. Many truck drivers and trucking companies will carry higher limits. Also, the truck and trailer may be separately registered and insured. This will double the amount of insurance money available to pay victims' claims. In catastrophic injury cases involving a commercial truck, always explore the assets of the truck driver and his or her employer and identify umbrella liability insurance or any additional commercial insurance coverage available to fund victim losses. The policy covering the truck is often only the first layer of insurance coverage and the $750,000.00 may be insufficient to cover a serious injury claim.

Another additional payment source in trucking cases would be the "hidden defendant." If the truck driver appears to be an independent owner-operator, careful investigation may reveal that he or she was employed by an outside entity. The company employing the driver may be held jointly liable for the victim's accident claims. If the collision arose from negligent maintenance and the maintenance facility is independent from the truck driver and his or her employer, the maintenance facility may also be held responsible for payment of accident claims. If the collision occurred because of a defective component on the truck (e.g., faulty brakes), the manufacturer of the truck or component part should be involved in the suit as well. Securing payment from all possible sources will allow the victim to receive the funds he or she truly needs to confront and overcome serious injuries.

During my years as an adjuster, I had occasion to work with the on-call adjusting team for the insurance company's trucking claims office. I saw firsthand how aggressively insurance carriers work to avoid responsibility for truck accidents. Insurance carriers ask truck drivers to report accident claims immediately from the collision scene. In fact, many truck drivers will report an accident to their insurance company before they call 911 to seek emergency assistance! In catastrophic cases, our adjusters would be paged and occasionally called to meet a chartered plane and fly in the middle of the night to an accident scene. Our orders were to secure statements from witnesses and victims to identify evidence that would allow us to reduce claims payments or deny victims' claims outright. Trucking accidents often result in very serious injuries. This factor, coupled with the high amount of mandatory insurance, motivates insurance carriers to prioritize these claims. They are typically slow to accept legal liability, and they work hard to avoid full responsibility for victims' losses.

The accident victim should also act immediately to protect all legal rights after an accident. The first few days following the truck accident can be critical. For example, if the truck driver is able to drive his or her truck after the collision, the speed and braking information recorded on the electronic control module (commonly referred to as the "black box") can be easily erased. Black box data is typically stored with a sudden braking event. Unfortunately, subsequent sudden braking will erase the accident data. Most accidents involve sufficient brake force and speed chance to cause data to be recorded, including the truck's speed during the minutes before the accident, cruise control and other settings, and the driver's braking effort and force/speed at impact. This evidence may be critical to prove collision facts and driver negligence. The black box download must be conducted by a qualified expert, and the truck should also be carefully inspected for safety and equipment violations. The trucking company and insurance company hope that the victim will not ask for the inspection and download. In almost every truck accident involving severe injury, the time and expense involved are justified and the victim should immediately demand and secure this evidence.

Online research will help you to identify the trucking company and explore the size and nature of their trucking operation. Also, the federal DOT number associated with that particular motor carrier (trucking company) will be listed on the police report. For information about an individual trucking company or a motor carrier authorized by the federal Department of Transportation to carry cargo across state lines, visit www.safersys.org. With the DOT number in hand, this site allows you to review the motor carrier's accident history, safety history, and insurance information. For further information on North Carolina truck accident law, visit **www.carolinatrucklawyer.com**.

Commercial Vehicle Accidents

Many businesses employ drivers to conduct their day-to-day operations. Our roads are clogged with delivery vans, taxicabs, and all types of business vehicles. In some cases, it will not be obvious that the responsible driver was driving a business vehicle or acting within the scope of employment when the collision occurred.

Our law firm handled one case for a woman who suffered a cervical fracture caused by a driver who ran a red light in downtown Raleigh in the early afternoon. The driver's only apparent source of insurance was the liability policy on his *privately owned* pickup truck. Our involvement and investigation forced disclosure of the responsible driver's points of origin and destination and the purpose of his journey. After learning that he was employed by a large retailer, we collected an additional $550,000.00 for the client above the $100,000.00 coverage on the at-fault driver's auto policy. This commercial coverage was hidden, and our client nearly accepted the $100,000.00 before we were retained. In serious injury cases, always look for hidden defendants and secondary insurance coverage.

Most businesses will carry liability insurance on all business vehicles and additional commercial liability insurance coverage to protect the business's assets. When a commercial vehicle is involved, we typically see high insurance coverage limits. Because the stakes are so high, the most skilled adjusters are employed to protect the insurance carrier. By aggressively pushing all medical evidence and damage claims, the victim can typically overcome adjuster opposition and secure generous settlement offers. Trial verdicts are typically higher in these cases because the business enterprise can be named as a party defendant. Juries seem more willing to grant larger verdicts because they feel that a large business is better able to afford to pay the full value of all losses resulting from a commercial vehicle accident.

Taxicabs are the only common exception to the expectation of high coverage limits in the commercial vehicle accident setting. While most business vehicles carry high coverage limits, most cab companies employ the driver as an independent contractor and thereby shield the company from joint liability. The cabdriver essentially owns a small, one-cab business that is not legally connected to the dispatcher or the cab company. We commonly see cabdrivers operating with the bare minimum amount of coverage required by the North Carolina Financial Responsibility Act.

Unfortunately, the independent contractor relationship will typically be upheld by the court. Therefore, the victim must look to his or her own underinsured motorist coverage under all applicable policies to secure additional compensation in most taxi accident cases.

If a business vehicle is involved, the victim should also explore the accident and safety history for the commercial driver *and* for the business enterprise. If the company operates a fleet of poorly maintained or dangerous vehicles, the victim may be able to collect additional compensation through a claim for punitive damages against the commercial enterprise. A jury may award these additional damages if they find that the commercial driver or the business willingly and knowingly endangered the public.

Drunk Driving and Punitive Damage Cases

If your accident was caused by a drunk driver, you should carefully consider whether punitive damages might be awarded as additional compensation for your injuries and experience. To collect punitive damages, you must show a willful decision to endanger others. You must also show that the driver will not be properly punished by the criminal courts. A first offender with a blood alcohol content just slightly above the legal limit likely would not be subject to a civil claim for punitive damages.

The courts look for a pattern of willful disregard of the rights and safety of other drivers before they will allow a punitive damage claim. In cases of extremely excessive speed, repeat offense drunk driving, racing, or other egregious conduct leading to accident and injury, a punitive damage claim should be presented. Proper investigation should include careful review of the police file and the criminal court's disposition of all charges arising from the accident. Also, a nationwide search of the responsible driver's past driving record and past criminal history is imperative.

At the time of trial or settlement discussions, a subsequent criminal record search is also imperative. Repeat offense drunk drivers will often commit subsequent offenses. If we can show that the drunk driver in your case willfully drove impaired again after your accident, this solidifies the claim for punitive damages.

The victim's right to claim punitive damages in North Carolina is governed purely by statute. Our punitive damage statute, N.C.G.S. 1D-35, provides as follows:

In determining the amount of punitive damages, if any, to be awarded, the trier of fact (jury):

(1) shall consider the purposes of punitive damages set forth in N.C.G.S. 1 D-1 (to punish a defendant for egregiously wrongful acts and to deter the defendant and others from committing similar wrongful acts); and

(2) may consider only that evidence that relates to the following:

    a. The reprehensibility of the defendant's motives and conduct.

    b. The likelihood, at the relevant time, of the defendant's conduct causing serious harm.

    c. The degree of the defendant's awareness of the probable consequences of his conduct.

    d. The duration of defendant's wrongful conduct.

    e. The actual damages suffered by the claimant/victim.

    f. Any concealment by the defendant of the facts or the consequences of his/her conduct.

    g. The existence and frequency of any similar past conduct by the defendant.

    h. Whether the defendant profited from the wrongful conduct.

    i. The defendant's ability to pay punitive damages as evidenced by his/her income, revenues, or net worth.

A punitive damage trial is different from a typical personal injury case based on claims of negligence. In the typical injury case, the victim cannot offer trial evidence of the defendant's wealth or assets. In the punitive damage setting, this evidence is allowed. While the North

Carolina appellate courts have not decided on this issue, we believe that a punitive damage trial should allow introduction into evidence of all insurance policies available to fund the verdict for the defendant's benefit. If insurance pays the punitive award, the defendant is not being punished. Admitting evidence of available insurance will help the jury determine the size of the verdict necessary to actually reach the defendant's personal funds. This legal maneuver should vastly increase the value of a punitive damage award. Also, this approach would ensure that the punishment hits the proper target.

Recent legislation has imposed a ceiling on the jury award of punitive damages. Pursuant to N.C.G.S. 1D-25, punitive damages are capped at the greater of three times the compensatory damages or $250,000.00, whichever is greater. If the jury grants a much higher punitive award, the judge will write the verdict down so the judgment imposed does not exceed the statutory limit.

Animal in the Road Accident

Most accidents involving animals are single-vehicle collisions. Animal avoidance accidents are very common, especially in rural areas where deer often cross the roadway. Unfortunately, the driver and passengers injured in accidents caused by animals have very limited rights.

To collect in a personal injury claim against a driver who swerves to avoid a dog, a deer, or any animal in the roadway, you *must* prove that the driver committed some error. Insurance companies commonly deny these claims. To collect for personal injury, the passenger must show that the driver was negligent. North Carolina appellate courts have routinely upheld jury verdicts that find that the driver who swerves to avoid an animal is acting as any reasonable and prudent driver would under those emergency circumstances. Even in violent, roll-over collisions involving catastrophic injury, the victim would not be able to recover for medical expenses and pain and suffering unless he or she can show that the driver made some slight mistake. Insurance adjusters act immediately to secure recorded/written testimony from the driver and all passengers. They hope that the passenger/victim will be willing to solely blame the animal in the roadway for the incident. They will then close your file and refuse payment on all injury claims.

If the driver was driving too fast before he or she first noticed the animal in the roadway, this error would allow victims to collect full payment for all injury claims. If the driver was not paying proper attention and didn't notice the animal soon enough or if the driver overreacted and made unsafe choices, this would also allow the victims to collect insurance benefits. On the other hand, if the driver responded properly to the animal in the roadway, passengers cannot collect money damages against the driver's policy through a personal injury claim.

If the owner of the animal can be identified, he or she can be pursued for payment of damages by all innocent victims. Owners of cows, horses, and other livestock are legally required to safely fence and contain these animals. If livestock escapes and enters the roadway, the driver and passengers can collect for property damage and personal injury. The burden of proof is on the victim to show that the owner failed to exercise reasonable care to properly contain the animals. These claims are presented against the owners of livestock and their homeowner's or farming insurance policies.

If a dog enters the roadway in an area that has a fence or leash law, the dog's owner can be pursued and most homeowner's policies carry a $300,000.00 liability policy, which would apply if a jury found that the dog's owner failed to comply with a legal duty to leash or otherwise contain his or her dog. However, if there is no law or local ordinance, current case law does not impose a legal duty on dog owners to fence or leash the dog. Thus, there would be no owner liability and therefore no avenue of recovery absent a showing of driver error. In all cases where the driver contributes to causing the accident involving an animal in the roadway, guest passengers can collect from the driver's liability insurance and all other underinsured motorist policies in his or her household.

Fatal Injury & Wrongful Death

Cases involving fatal injury involve many complex legal issues. These are also difficult cases for the family to face and present. Multiple family members typically share the right to compensation in cases involving death of a loved one, and the surviving family members must fully understand North Carolina's Wrongful Death Act and all of the damages laws, estate and probate laws, and tax laws that affect the case.

Under North Carolina law, a wrongful death claim can be presented whenever a person's death is caused by the wrongful act, neglect or fault of another. The Wrongful Death Act is the statute that establishes the right to present fatal injury claims, and allows surviving family members to collect for collision related financial and emotional losses. The intended purpose of the Wrongful Death Act is to financially place the legal beneficiaries of the deceased victim in the same position that they would have been had the victim not died.

The surviving family members must be equipped to present all evidence relating both to the cause of death, and also to prove all emotional and financial losses imposed upon the family due to the decedent's passing. Although a human life can never be replaced, the devastating financial consequences caused by the loss of a loved one can be lessened if all responsible parties are compelled to pay fair value for the lost income, lost companionship, and all lost household contributions of the victim.

Elements of a Wrongful Death Claim

If a fatal injury is caused by another's negligent or careless conduct, the burden of proof in the civil trial necessary to collect for wrongful death damages in North Carolina is "preponderance of the evidence". Under North Carolina law, "preponderance of evidence" simply means a slight tipping of the scales. Put another way, the plaintiff must show that the allegation asserted is "more likely than not" true.

All of the negligence laws discussed throughout this book apply win the wrongful death context. Claimants in the wrongful death action must prove that other drivers' or parties' errors caused the fatal injury, and most of the accident case is presented just as if the victim had survived. Because wrongful death actions are based on statutory law, the claim must be in conformity with the requirements of the North Carolina Wrongful Death Act, codified in North Carolina General Statutes 28A-18-2. The elements of a wrongful death claim include the classic elements of a negligence case, plus additional proof required to show:

1. the full financial value of losses incurred by the family;
2. the emotional loss and quality of all relationships affected; and
3. the identity and family standing of all beneficiaries entitled to share in any wrongful death settlement.

Proving & Collecting All Damages

The most critical task involved in securing fair compensation for wrongful death is application of all evidence laws and the law of damages to ensure that all losses arising from the fatality are properly established and paid in full. Once all responsible parties are identified, and once all applicable insurance policies are located and brought in to maximize available coverage/funds, the goal is to secure the highest possible settlement or verdict for surviving family members.

The damages that are recoverable in a lawsuit for wrongful death are specified in the Wrongful Death Act. These include:

1. Expenses for care, treatment and hospitalization related to the injury that resulted in death;
2. Compensation for pain and suffering of the decedent;
3. The reasonable funeral expenses of the decedent;
4. The present monetary value of the decedent to the persons entitled to receive the damages recovered, including but not limited to compensation for the loss of the reasonably expected:
   a. Net income of the decedent,

b. Services, protection, care and assistance of the decedent, whether voluntary or obligatory, to the persons entitled to the damages recovered;

c. Society, companionship, comfort, guidance, kindly offices and advice of the decedent to the persons entitled to the damages recovered;

5. Such punitive damages as the decedent could have recovered pursuant to Chapter 1D of the General Statutes had he survived, and punitive damages for wrongfully causing the death of the decedent through malice or willful or wanton conduct, as defined in N.C.G.S. 1D-5.

In the following paragraphs, we explore important issues pertaining to each category of collectable loss:

Collecting All Medical Costs:

Evidence proving the decedent's medical expenses and funeral expenses will be straightforward and requires only the tender of the specific invoices. North Carolina evidence law was revised several years ago and these revisions dramatically reduce the amount of medical charges that can be claimed in most personal injury cases. Under the new law, evidence of medical expenses is limited to the actual amount paid, regardless of source, plus any amount that remains due to fully satisfy the bill. This law only limits the rights of victims with health insurance, and the effect is to reduce the amount of bills admitted for payment. If the health insurance carrier is entitled to discounts or "adjustments" which reduce the total bill, then this reduced amount (or amount "actually paid") is the only amount that can be recovered in a North Carolina wrongful death case. If the decedent had no health insurance, the total bill can be presented for payment. Obviously, this would increase the total value of the wrongful death claim. We hope to see constitutional challenge of this law because victims who had health insurance are clearly denied equal protection under the current law.

Collecting for Pain & Suffering:

The N.C. Wrongful Death Act allows the victim's family to collect payment for the pain and suffering of the decedent. To collect for pain and suffering in a wrongful death case, the Plaintiff must prove that the victim was aware or conscious of their pain and suffering. Attorneys typically rely on medical experts in cases of rapid death to show that, even if for merely a few seconds, the decedent was fearful and aware of physical pain and injury. In most cases, if the victim evidenced obvious pain and difficulty before death, or if the victim lingers with their injuries and struggles for life before passing, it is easy to show that conscious pain and suffering occurred. Generally, if there is no time interval between injury and death, as when the victim is instantly killed with no awareness of the circumstance, there can be no recovery of damages for pain and suffering. Evidence of pain and suffering can be established through medical records, testimony of witnesses who observed or heard the defendant, and from the dying declarations of the victim.

Collecting for Lost Income:

The N.C. Wrongful Death Act allows claimants to collect the lost "net income" of the decedent. The goal here is to collect all lost wages that would have been earned by the victim over the course of an uninterrupted, normal life. Lawyers refer to this as a "lifetime earnings claim". In money value, this means that the surviving family can collect the decedent's total lost future income from all sources, reduced by the amount that would be due for taxes. The total lifetime income stream is first calculated, and then this amount must be reduced to the present monetary value.

The sources of recoverable lost income include salary, fringe benefits, commissions, retirement accounts, and all other foreseeable income that the decedent would have earned. Only those amounts that would have gone to or been available for the beneficiaries, but for the wrongful death, are recoverable. The relevant factors on which these damage calculations are based include the decedent's life expectancy, health and habits, employment, education, training, career path and earning history.

The surviving family members or their attorney should always work closely with vocational rehabilitation experts and economic experts to show the likely earning capacity of the victim, and to show a jury the <u>full</u> amount that the family will miss in earnings due to the fatal accident. The vocational expert will investigate trends in earnings and project the career path and future earnings that the decedent likely would have earned over their lifetime. The economic expert will refine those figures, put a reliable dollar figure on the total future income stream, and then reduce the total of all lost income to a single lump sum stated in "present monetary value". This figure is the exact sum that would have to be placed in an interest-bearing bank account today to provide the family with the same income stream they would have enjoyed if the victim had not been fatally injured.

<u>Collecting for Lost Services, Protection & Care:</u>

The family of a fatal accident victim can also collect compensation for the value of all "services, protection, care and assistance of the decedent, whether voluntary or obligatory, to the persons entitled to the damages recovered." This subcategory of damages provides additional money, beyond lost income, for the services that the victim could have performed if he or she had survived. Typical damages in this category include the value of tasks involved in maintaining the household such as cooking, cleaning, caring for children, yard maintenance, household chores and maintenance, and performing general errands. Since outsiders can be employed to fill these roles, these services have a monetary value that can be calculated and reduced to present value.

Proof of the full value of all lost services as reduced to present monetary value can be complex. In general, it is advisable to employ an expert economist to assist in the itemization and calculation of these damages. Insurance companies always question damage claims, and the involvement of an expert will confirm the true value of all damages and your readiness to proceed through trial if necessary to secure full and fair compensation.

<u>Collecting for Lost Companionship & Relationship</u>:

The N.C. Wrongful Death Act also allows the victim's family to collect fair compensation for the "[s]ociety, companionship, comfort, guidance, kindly offices and advice of the decedent to the persons entitled to the damages recovered." Because the lost relationship and companionship is intangible, these claims are very difficult to quantify. Trial attorneys agree that jurors are often quite sympathetic in death cases, and they are often moved toward generosity when they hear of the relationships that are lost due to fatal accidents. However, valuing this portion of the case is difficult as many people disagree on how to value a lost life. Loss of society and companionship is intangible, and the Wrongful Death Act here seeks to compensate the surviving family members for the sense of loss, heartache and anguish resulting from the fatality. Evidence of a close and loving family with details of the relationship and good times enjoyed is relevant and admissible in trial.

In the settlement setting, it is best to put together a presentation that illuminates the decedent's persona and character, and that clearly shows how much the decedent will be missed by all surviving family members. A proper settlement demand brochure should include photographs, family videos, letters and statements of friends and family members, hobbies shared and anything the decedent created, and any credentials that show the decedent's interests, accomplishments and character. Even in distant families, efforts should be made to show how the decedent will be missed, and to prove the weight and value of the loss of life. These materials will all be relevant and admissible at trial if the case cannot be resolved through private compromise.

<u>Collecting Punitive Damages</u>:

The Wrongful Death Act allows the recovery of punitive damages if the victim could have recovered a punitive award if he or she had survived. Unlike all other elements of the wrongful death claim, the Plaintiff's burden on the level of the defendant's wrongful conduct is proof by "clear and convincing evidence". The conduct involved must be severely wrongful. Therefore, it must be clear and convincing to a jury that the defendant's conduct that caused the fatal injury was malicious, willful or wanton, or grossly negligent. Under N.C. law, these terms are defined as follows:

- Malicious Act - an act is malicious when the defendant was motivated by personal ill will or spite.
- Willful Act - an act is willful if the defendant intentionally fails to carry out some duty imposed by law or contract which is necessary to protect the safety of the person or property to which the duty is owed.
- Wanton Conduct - an act is wanton if the defendant acts in conscious or reckless disregard for the rights and safety of others.
- Gross Negligence - an act is grossly negligent when the defendant lacks even slight care, when he shows indifference to the rights and welfare of others, or when his negligence is of an aggravated character

For further information about how a punitive damage claim is valued and presented, see the Punitive Damage Claims discussion which begins on page 211. The same approach taken in a punitive damage claim involving non-fatal injury applies in a punitive damage claim that is attached to a wrongful death action. The only difference is that, in fatal accident cases, gross negligence (which is a lower level of wrongdoing than intentional, malicious, or willful and wanton conduct) is sufficient to support a claim for punitive damages when the grossly negligent conduct results in fatality.

The Role of the Estate Representative

It is vitally important to promptly open an estate and secure appointment of the legal representative of the estate. Even if the decedent died without any assets, an Estate file must be opened naming a Personal Representative in order for a wrongful death claim to be maintained.

A claim for wrongful death can only be brought by the "Personal Representative" of the decedent – either the Administrator (if the decedent died without a will) or the Executor/Executrix (if the decedent died with a will naming an Executor). The Personal Representative has the exclusive right to initiate and file a wrongful death claim, to the exclusion of beneficiaries, heirs, legatees, or survivors. Please note, however, that even though it is the Personal Representative who brings the claim, it is the beneficiaries or surviving family members who receive the case proceeds.

How Family Members Divide a Wrongful Death Award

The family members who have a right to share in the wrongful death proceeds are exactly the same family members who would receive assets from the decedent's estate if the decedent died with no valid will at the time of death. The North Carolina Intestate Succession Act is the law that provides for the distribution of a decedent's assets in cases where a N.C. citizen dies with no valid will. This statute also identifies exactly who would collect from a wrongful death settlement or trial verdict. Further, even if the decedent had a will, the will does not effect the list of parties who collect in the wrongful death case. Thus, even if the victim was estranged and entirely out of touch with a surviving family member, and even if that family member was intentionally excluded from the decedent's written will, the excluded family member still has a right to a share of the wrongful death proceeds in North Carolina.

For the complete law of intestate succession, see N.C.G.S. Chapter 29. The following is a summary of how wrongful death case proceeds are paid out to surviving family members:

If the decedent was married at the time of wrongful death:

- Spouse surviving and no children or descendants of children surviving & no parent surviving – All funds to spouse.
- Spouse surviving and no children or descendants of children surviving & one/both parents surviving– First $100,000.00 to spouse and remaining proceeds divided in half between spouse and surviving parent(s).
- Spouse surviving and one child or descendants of one child also surviving– First $60,000.00 to spouse and remaining proceeds

divided in half between spouse and surviving child or descendants of non-surviving child.

- Spouse surviving and two or more children or their descendants– First $60,000.00 to spouse, one-third of remaining proceeds to spouse and two-thirds of remaining proceeds to children or descendants.

If the decedent was single at the time of wrongful death:

- If children or decedents are alive – All proceeds to child(ren) or descendants of child(ren).
- Parent(s) surviving but decedent had no children – All proceeds of wrongful death claim paid to parents.
- Brother(s) or sister(s) surviving, no children or surviving parent – All proceeds shared by surviving sibling(s) and their descendants. See N.C.G.S. 29-15(4) & 29-16(6) for complete explanation of shares of descendants.
- No children or their descendants, no parents, no siblings or sibling descendants – One-half to paternal grandparents but, if not surviving, then to paternal Uncles, Aunts or their descendants. Remaining one-half to maternal grandparents but, if not surviving, then to maternal Uncles, Aunts or their descendants.

If any person entitled to distribution of wrongful death proceeds is a minor (under the age of eighteen years), then any settlement of a wrongful death claim must be approved by the Court through an action filed by the minor's Guardian ad Litem. Wrongful death proceeds for minor children can also be placed into annuities through structured settlements to ensure that the child's funds earn interest over time, and to allow the family to divide case payments so the child at age 18 is not faced with the sudden responsibility of handling the total case payout at such a young age. Minor settlements are discussed in further detail beginning on page 187, and the structured settlement process is outlined beginning on page 189.

Wrongful Death Case Defenses

North Carolina law provides that the claim for wrongful death is "derivative" of the victim's rights. Thus, it derives from the same rights the decedent would have had he/she survived. Thus, a wrongful death claim can be presented only if the injured person would have had a claim for their injuries, had they lived. Any and all defenses the defendant would have to such a lawsuit brought by the injured person will also be available in a wrongful death action brought by the estate's Personal Representative. While some defenses reduce case value, others end the case and terminate all payment rights.

Insurance companies and their lawyers <u>always</u> work to either reduce case value or to avoid payment obligations entirely by bringing forward every legal defense available under North Carolina law. Regardless of the tragic nature of fatal accidents, the defense will look only at their own legal and financial interests. Wrongful death defendants are allowed to assert all of the same defenses available in general civil lawsuits. These legal defenses include procedural defenses that bar all claims, such as lack of jurisdiction, failure to state a proper legal claim, or failure to file the lawsuit within the deadline imposed by the statute of limitations

The defense will also challenge liability and seek to avoid legal responsibility for the fatal accident. Claimants in wrongful death actions should be particularly mindful of North Carolina's pure contributory negligence law. Under this law, a N.C. wrongful death claimant cannot collect if the defense can show that the decedent contributed even slightly (just 1%) to causing the accident or injuries that resulted in death. Because wrongful death claims are typically quite valuable, the most experienced insurance adjusters are assigned to these cases and they begin working immediately after the claim is reported to locate and preserve evidence supporting this defense.

Insurance carriers in these cases typically cherry-pick the financial claims, and dispute the amount of future income that might have been earned by the decedent. They also will not hesitate to challenge the quality of family relationships. In fact, claims adjusters and insurance defense lawyers often look for ways to attack the character of the decedent. If you anticipate and stand ready for this approach, you will be properly prepared to meet the defense head-on with evidence which would show a jury that quality relationships have been lost, and that the decedent was a person of true value to the family.

Wrongful Death Case Filing Deadline

The statute of limitations in North Carolina for a wrongful death claim is two years, which is measured from the date of the victim's death. This is the deadline for filing the lawsuit against all people and businesses who share responsibility for the fatal accident. Further, because the action is derivative of the decedent's rights, the wrongful death lawsuit must be filed and properly initiated in the proper court within the same time period during which the victim could have brought a claim for injuries, had they lived. If the action would be barred by the statute of limitations if the victim were still alive and had sued, then a wrongful death claim based on the same injuries is also barred by the statute of limitations. For example, if an accident victim is injured in an accident and survives for more than three years and during the fourth year dies from the same injuries, the claim would be time-barred by the applicable three year statute of limitations for negligence actions.

In rare cases, the statute of limitations may be "tolled", or delayed, such that the claim could be brought more than two years after the victim's death. For example, in cases where there was no estate administered because the decedent left no property, but had a minor child, it is possible that the child's claim for the wrongful death of the parent would be tolled until the child reached 18, which is the age of majority in North Carolina. Thus, the two year period would begin to run only after the child was a legal adult able to bring legal action on his/her own behalf.

Legal deadlines imposed by the statute of limitations are strict deadlines that can eliminate all legal rights to compensation arising from a fatal accident. Determining the exact suit-filing deadline can be tricky in some cases, especially where death is delayed or where no estate is filed and young children survive the decedent. Always seek direct advice on case deadlines from an experienced wrongful death lawyer as soon as possible in all wrongful death cases. Even if you choose to handle the fatal accident case without counsel, you should allow a trial lawyer to consider your family's unique circumstances and provide reliable deadlines for all legal filings.

How to Divide and Pay Out Wrongful Death Funds

The Wrongful Death Act spells out the proper priority of payment of all case proceeds as follows:

- First, any expenses advanced by the estate for costs associated with prosecution of the wrongful death case are paid back to the estate.
- Second, attorney's fees are paid from the settlement or verdict.
- Third, burial expenses of the deceased are paid, and reasonable hospital and medical expenses not exceeding $4500 incident to the injury resulting in death are paid, except that the amount applied for hospital and medical expenses shall not exceed 50% of the amount of damages recovered after deducting attorney's fees.
- Fourth, the full remaining balance is then distributed to surviving family according to the Intestate Succession Act as if the decedent died without a will, even if in fact he or she did have a will.

Unlike other bank accounts or assets owned by the decedent at the time of death, the wrongful death case proceeds do not become part of the "estate assets". Attorneys who handle these claims describe the approach by stating that wrongful death proceeds are paid "outside of the estate". This is very beneficial because a large award would not be reduced even if the decedent died with large debts or outside financial obligations. Simply put, the surviving family members keep the wrongful death proceeds and they do not have to pay any estate debts or taxes, except for the burial and hospital expenses mentioned.

Wrongful death claims are subject to health insurance lien claims, including claims asserted by publicly funded health insurance such as Medicaid and Medicare. Because the laws pertaining to government claims against wrongful death proceeds are constantly evolving, you should secure an up-to-date legal opinion on the validity and value of outside claims at the time of settlement or trial. Health insurance reimbursement claims can be discounted and, through aggressive negotiations, considerable money can be saved for the benefit of surviving family members.